ENGLISH
FOR THE
DISENCHANTED

Ruth Townsend
Yorktown High School
Yorktown Heights, New York

Marcia Lubell
Yorktown High School
Yorktown Heights, New York

SOUTH-WESTERN
PUBLISHING CO.

Executive Editor: Carol Lynne Ruhl
Acquisitions Editor: Janie F. Schwark
Production Editor: Joseph P. Powell III
Designer: Nicola M. Jones
Marketing Manager: Al S. Roane

ISBN: 0-538-60995-8

Library of Congress Catalog Card Number: 91-62144

2 3 4 5 6 D 98 97 96 95 94 93 92

Printed in the United States of America

EPIGRAPH

I sat alone in the classroom a long time. I listened to the boys outside, down-stairs, shouting and cursing and laughing. Their laughter struck me for perhaps the first time. It was not the joyous laughter which—God know why—one associates with children. It was mocking and insular, its intent was to denigrate. It was disenchanted, and in this, also, lay the authority of their curses.

"Sonny's Blues" by James Baldwin

PREFACE

Before we began our teaching careers many years ago, we believed that our commitment to teaching the language and literature we loved would be enough to enchant our students. We envisioned classes of teenagers readily succumbing to the power of language and the spell of literature. But that, as we said, was *before* we began teaching.

The disillusioning truth is that many of our students, even those in affluent suburban high schools, were disaffected with the traditional English/language arts programs we were teaching. Our students seemed to find no relevance to their own experiences in the programs that had constituted the English curriculum in the past. Even more widespread than the disengagement we discovered among our mainstream, middle-class students was the indifference of our students from culturally divergent backgrounds toward traditional English/language arts programs. These students—whose race, religion, language, or family traditions differed from white, European culture—found even less relevance to their lives in such programs. We tried to adapt traditional approaches to appeal to these uninvolved, often disconnected students, but, more often than not our efforts failed.

Unwilling to live with our failures, we decided to redesign our teaching strategies and our classroom practices to engage these uninterested students. We realized that our first task was to dispel the myth that "English" is a secret skill, the knowledge of which belongs only to the exclusive club of English teachers and honor students. It seemed obvious to us that if we were to overcome this misconception of English/language arts and open the doors of the "club" to our disenchanted students, we would have to acknowledge the social contexts to which they could relate. The results of our efforts are learning units we now offer to other teachers who may be experiencing some of the same frustrations we have had in working with disenchanted students.

The basis of our approach is engagement. We do this by tapping our students' natural enjoyment of competition and by appealing to their interests, experiences, and sense of humor. We have learned that without this engagement we can teach them nothing. With it, we can teach them the skills they must have to survive in an increasingly complex world. These survival skills include reading, writing, speaking, listening— the same skills of the traditional English/language arts classroom. What is different, however, is that they are woven into discrete learning units that involve problem solving, map reading, career planning, résumé writing, and other practical skills necessary for daily life. All of the learning projects within each unit are dependent upon collaborative learning procedures. At the same time, each unit provides students with opportunities to build on their individual interests, experiences, cultural identities, and strengths and to share them with each other. In this way, students learn from one another and begin to respect what each can contribute to their growth and development.

Some of the units contain fewer suggestions for integrating specific literary works into them than others. This is by design, not because we believe that literature is of secondary importance in the English/language arts curriculum, but so that each teacher can select literature best suited to his or her own students. The units are not meant to be a plan for a complete curriculum, nor are they geared to a particular secondary grade level. Rather, they are approaches for engaging students on several different grade levels and with various abilities in language activities. In each of the units different kinds of literature enhance the basic design. We have tried to select literature of generally recognized literary merit that students are likely to have some interest in and that reflects the diversity of the American culture. Each unit contains suggestions for teaching English language skills, along with the skills of critical literacy: comparing, synthesizing, and analyzing. We believe that within each unit teachers will find many opportunities to adapt and augment these model lessons, inspired by their own creativity in response to their disenchanted students.

CONTENTS

UNIT 7
HELP WANTED

Students read help-wanted columns, write responses, draft résumés, practice interviews, and research career opportunities.

UNIT 8
SHOW ME A STORY

Students read a variety of short stories, most of them contemporary, as a springboard for their own writing. Using dialogue and narrative descriptions from short stories, students create their own dramatized video versions.

UNIT 9
TRIALS AND TRIBULATIONS

Students research school and community concerns, learn about local resources and programs in which they can play a role, conduct interviews with and write letters to town and school officials on real problems, and explore issues in literature, for which they prepare and conduct trials before a jury of their peers.

THIS IS YOUR LIFE

I'm nobody! Who are you?
Are you nobody, too?
Then there's a pair of us—don't tell!
They'd banish us, you know.

How dreary to be somebody!
How public, like a frog.
To tell your name the livelong day
To an admiring bog!
                              Emily Dickinson

One of our first tasks as English teachers is to gain the trust of our students so that we can teach essential communication skills. Gaining the trust of "disenchanted students" can be particularly difficult, for these are the students who are predisposed to feeling alienated from formal classroom instruction. For them English has no relevance or interest. Like the speaker in Emily Dickinson's poem, they are the "nobodies" in the traditional English classroom, the detached students who have built a shell against anticipated failure. By the time they are in high school, their disengagement manifests itself as indifference to learning.

We designed "This Is Your Life" to help us create the kind of positive, comfortable environment necessary for success with this or any other student population. The basis of that success is the interest students have in finding out about themselves.

A primary goal of this unit is to enable students to understand themselves better, to know who they are as individuals.

To begin, we rely on their inherent fascination with self and explore with them the meanings of their given names. (See the addendum at the end of the chapter for an alternative approach that uses students' astrological signs.) This activity requires research on our parts. We get our class list several days before school begins and then determine the story behind each student's name: its origin, its historical background, and its meaning in religion, mythology, and literature. *What to Name Your Baby* by Maxwell Nurnberg and Morris Rosenblum, (Collier Books, 1984), and *Pocket Dictionary of Saints,* by John J. Delaney (Doubleday, 1983) are helpful for this task.

We begin to stimulate students' interest by asking them if they know what their names mean. Most of them don't. We say, "There is magic in your name.

Your name is what you are; it includes your past, present and future. It can even influence what you do with your life." Dramatic stuff, but engaging.

We share with them the results of our research into each of their names and tell them that Americans have a rich heritage of names from cultures and traditions all over the world. And we add, because it is always true, "From our research, we have discovered that you are unique and fascinating people."

We instruct the students to jot down what they learn about their individual names, assuring them they will need this information later.

As we read each name and share something about its meaning, we hold the attention of everyone. No need here to *ask* for their attention. Everyone is interested in what the names mean. For instance, a good deal of friendly laughter and ribbing occurs when we tell Jerome that his name is from the Greek, meaning "the holy name," and that some famous Jeromes in history include Saint Girolamo, a hermit and scholar who became one of the fathers of the Christian church, and the Native American chief Geronimo, whose name was the jumping cry of paratroopers in World War II.

Amy already knew that her name was from the Latin and means "the beloved." But she did not know that *Amy* came into popular use in English because of Saint Aimée of France, whose name was carried into England by the Normans in 1066, or that the Puritans brought the name to New England as *Amiable*, which means "virtue." Anyone named Amy has a great deal to live up to.

And so we go down the list of names, answering questions, as we can—especially about the lives (more often the ghastly deaths) of the saints whose names many students share. All this takes time, but we believe it is well worth it. Not only are the students getting to know each other, but we are building rapport with them, demonstrating our interest in them, and showing our appreciation of their uniqueness.

After we have completed the class list, we ask the students to consider what we have told them about their names (remember, we had them take notes) and to write us a letter about how well they fit the legacy of their names. Perhaps they see themselves as completely different from what their names suggest, or perhaps they are startled to find how well they fit the picture painted by the history of their names. We ask them to go into some detail as they agree or disagree with the aptness of their names in relation to their own personalities.

We then read what our students have written and respond promptly with personal comments and observations. We do not make corrections of any kind, for our purpose here is to encourage them to share their thoughts with us, to open lines of communication, and to assess the strengths and weaknesses of their compositions. We remember at this point in the course that our primary goal is to create a climate of trust and to show our students the relevance of what we do in English class to their personal lives. We also instruct them to bring journals to class every day because they will be writing in them regularly.

To begin we ask our students to think of all experiences that affected them in a significant way and to write about one of these in their journals. To give them an idea of what to do, we model the journal writing process. Marcia tells the class about an experience of performing at a piano recital that affected her life:

Every time I think of performing in front of an audience, my skin crawls and I can feel fear gnaw at the pit of my stomach. Will I disgrace myself again? Will I forget?

I can still remember one particularly dreadful piano recital. Every year for 12 miserable years, as predictible as spring showers, I'd get dressed in my stiffly starched white recital dress and march into the Wood Auditorium with my beaming parents, my grandparents, my sister, and God knows who else they had dragged along.

This particular Sunday afternoon was stifling. The crowd looked huge as I gazed around the room. I felt the hum and buzz of the preconcert crowd engulf me, and my knees buckled as I dreamt of precipitous flight. I longed to be anywhere but here. What on earth was I doing here anyway? I was no musician. Lord knows I tried. I dutifully practiced two hours every day, seemingly forever, but I never got much better. As long as I played for myself, with music, I was tolerable. But here? By memory? For all these people? I looked at the people around me, all smiling, seemingly happy to be there. I bet they didn't even like music. I bet they didn't want to be here any more than I did!

I was fourth on the program. What an interminable wait. I sat in the front row, my eyes glassy, my hands clammy, desperation oozing from every pore. Everybody else played *so* well! That only made me feel more terrified. I was really getting myself into a state.

Finally it was my turn. As I walked up to the huge Steinway, I stumbled and almost fell; I heard a hush in the audience. I started to play. It was going to be all right. My fingers were going to carry me through, even if my memory couldn't. But suddenly my mind wandered, and I forgot the next part; my hands froze on the keyboard. Oh, no! What was I going to do? All my worst fears were coming true. Never, never have I been so mortified, felt so stupid. My face flushed red; my spine tingled with electric shock.

Suddenly, by some miracle, the music appeared in front of me. I was rescued. I made it through the piece, and the crowd was more than generous with its applause. But I staggered off the stage as fast as I could, humiliated.

Instead of returning to my seat, I ran out of the auditorium through the back entrance. Never again, I thought, never again will I put myself through anything like that!

After we have modeled the assignment, we direct our students to write about their experience and include what they were like both before the experience and after it. We allow plenty of time for them to think about an experience and write about it. We move around the room, encouraging those who are having difficulty thinking of an incident. To stimulate their memory, we ask such questions as: "Were you ever embarrassed? Did you ever forget something important? Did you ever make a terrible mistake? Did you ever lose anything of value? Were you ever unfairly punished? Have you ever been frightened? Did you ever win an award? Did you ever do something you were especially proud of? Did you ever accomplish something you didn't think you were capable of?" If students can answer yes to any of these questions, we instruct them to jot down the details of the incident and tell how they were affected by the event.

Next we ask students to find a partner with whom to share their recollections of the experience that affected them in a significant way. Students are not to read from their journal entry but simply to retell the incident. First, one person shares his or her incident for about two minutes. The second person then shares his or her incident. We ask students to jot down what they recall about the experience their partners shared with them. They review these notes with each other to see how well they listened. At this point partners may confer for a few more minutes and get additional information about each other's experience to add to their notes.

We invite each pair to join with another pair to form groups of four students. These students review their notes and, without looking at the notes, introduce their partners to the other members of the group by relating the experience that affected that partner in a significant way.

The value of this experience is in the interactive climate it encourages in the classroom. While the students are talking to each other, they are employing language skills that are important for them to learn. In this one exercise alone they have practiced journal writing, note taking, listening, and speaking. In addition, they have reflected on the impact of an important event on their own lives, as well as the significance of similar events on the lives of their classmates. This type of exercise can be done on a variety of different topics as the students begin to explore what is important to them and the problems they face in coping with everyday life. Some of the events they have shared with their classmates include embarrassing moments, conflicts with family, academic and athletic achievements, and brushes with death.

For instance, Elizabeth told about her problem with sibling rivalry:

My dad walked through the front door with a big smile on his face. Behind him was my mom holding a bundle of blankets, which she placed on the couch.

"Liz, come and look what we brought from the hospital," said my mom, unwrapping the blankets.

I walked over to the couch hesitantly to look at a squirming baby.

"You have a new baby brother," exclaimed my dad, leaning over to kiss him.

I reached out to touch his fingers, but he began to cry. My mom rushed over and grabbed him off the couch. She sat down in the rocking chair and began to rock and sing to him the way she used to to me. He soon fell asleep and she placed him in the crib. My mom sighed and sat down on the couch. She looked tired.

I went over to the crib and I watched him. He was so quiet and peaceful. I wanted to touch him so I reached out to pet his head. All of a sudden his little head popped up and he began to cry again.

"Liz. Don't touch the baby while he is sleeping!" yelled my mom.

My mom never yelled at me so I ran into my room and closed the door. I folded my arms across my chest and sat in the corner of my bed.

"All that baby does is cry. My mom doesn't hold me and sing to me anymore. Why do I have to have a little brother?" I said to myself.

I wanted to put my pajamas on and go to bed, but I needed help taking off my shirt. I pulled it over my head and I got stuck.

"Mom, come here!" I called.

"I can't. I am feeding the baby."

"But I'm stuck." I screamed.

I started to cry, but finally I got my shirt off by myself. My mom wouldn't even help me get unstuck.

I walked out into the t.v. room where my mom and dad were playing with the baby.

I sat down next to them, but they acted like I wasn't even there. Frustrated I got up and went to bed without kissing them goodnight.

The next morning I was in the t.v. room watching Bugs Bunny and then I heard a knock on the door. It was Grandma and Grandpa.

"Oh, hi, dear," said Grandma patting me on the head as she walked by.

Grandpa had a bunch of presents in his arms and they walked over to my mom, who was holding that baby again. They fussed over who would get to hold him. I tugged on my Grandpa's pant leg, but he wouldn't even look down at me. I was really getting angry. All of a sudden I pinched him and ran. He yelled and dropped the present that he was handing to my mother. My dad ran after me, grabbed me and spanked me. I was too mad to cry. I just wanted somebody to play with me.

Since nobody cared anything about me I went into my room and took out some crayons. I drew a picture of the baby. I gave him a monster's face. Then I ripped it up because I was afraid my mom wouldn't like that. Just then my mom came in and sat down on the bed next to me.

"What's the matter with you?" she asked picking up the paper on the floor.

"Nobody cares about me anymore. You and dad are always with that baby. I don't want a little brother. Could we send him back where he came from?"

"No we can't. The baby is too little to do things on his own. Now you are a big girl and you can feed yourself, go to the bathroom, and dress yourself. Your daddy and I love you just as much as we ever did," explained my mommy.

We went into the kitchen and she put the baby's bottle in my hand. She sat me down on the couch and placed the baby in my arms. I put the bottle in his mouth and his big brown eyes looked right at me. He finished his bottle and my mom took him from me, put him over her shoulder to make him burp; then I watched him lying there next to the stuffed bear that Grandma gave him. Because the playpen was big enough, I climbed in. I sat him up in my lap and held him and this time he didn't cry. Then I knew why I had a little brother. It was so I could love him.

We follow up with one or both of the following activities. The first activity is designed for the more able students, those capable of sustaining interest in an introspective discussion. The second follow-up works best with students who need a more concrete, physically active experience.

In the first activity each student is asked to discover more about the incidents that affected the other three members of her or his group. To help students elicit enough information about the experiences so that they can write about them, we have the class brainstorm on the kinds of questions that could be asked. Sample questions generated by students include: "What were you like before this experience? When did it occur? Where? What else happened? Who else was involved? What did you do? Think? Feel? Say? What were you like afterward? What about it caused you to change? How is this change reflected in what you now do?"

To gather this information, students remain in their groups of four and interview each other. For a homework assignment students are asked to write about the interviews in their journals. We read the journals, assessing them only as they reveal students' strengths and weaknesses in written expression. We neither correct nor comment on errors in form and language mechanics. We respond only to content, remarking on what we find particularly interesting or what we wish we knew more about, commending them for the completeness or liveliness of their accounts. Our purpose at this stage in the course is to promote a comfortable classroom environment, one in which students feel free to share personal experiences and write their reactions without fear of negative criticism. We provide opportunities later in the course for students to develop finished pieces of writing.

For the second activity we encourage students to think about what is important to them, their values. We then list the values identified by the students. They usually include family, tradition, wealth, love, health, wisdom, knowledge, power, peace, truth, happiness, and friendship. We ask the students to list in their journals three of their most important values and explain the reasons for their choices. We organize students into groups of four, making sure the groups are balanced in terms of ability. The groups look through popular magazines to find visual representations of their values and create "values collages" from the pictures. After they write an explanation for their collages, we exhibit them on the bulletin boards all around the room.

Again as a class, we discuss the values and write on the board those mentioned most often. We add to the list of values until we have approximately 20. Now we explain to our students that they have an opportunity to create a new civilization. They will be transported to a new planet, where, based upon their values, they will create a unique society. To determine what values each group has, we will hold a "values auction." (Our inspiration for this activity was Sidney B. Simon's book *Values Clarification: A Handbook of Practical Strategies for Teachers and Students.* Hart Publishing Co., 1972.) Each group imagines it has $1,000 to spend on purchasing the values the class has selected. The bidding begins at $50 and continues in increments of $50. Either a student or one of us functions as auctioneer. Before the auction begins, students meet in groups to discuss which values are most important to the whole group and how much they are willing to pay for each value. They need to budget the money they have been allotted and to create a priority list for the values on which they wish to bid. We suggest that they will need at least three values in order to create their society.

The auction itself, for which we allow a full class period, tends to be a very loud, funny, totally engaging event. Students throw themselves into activities like this with great fervor, acting as though getting the values they want is a life-or-death matter. Once the auction is over each group should have at least three values, if things have worked out smoothly. Occasionally a group will rashly bid all its money on one value—such as money or power—whereupon the challenge for them is very great as they try to complete the follow-up activity successfully.

Before students begin to create their societies, we brainstorm as a class on the elements that characterize any society. Students usually mention its economic system, government, foreign relations, defense, and culture, including family, religion, and education. Then they work in their several groups to determine how their values will affect each of these categories.

Each group's first task is to work out a general philosophy for its society based on their values. We take this opportunity to examine documents that reflect national philosophies. We begin with the American Declaration of Independence and the Bill of Rights. The students read these documents in their groups and identify the values reflected in them. As a class, we discuss the results of the group examinations. Students can easily recognize respect for the rights of the individual as the core of America's philosophy. We usually have to point out that the value placed on individual freedom is limited by the value placed on each citizen's responsibility for the welfare of the nation. We emphasize that this philosophy of respect for the individual and the welfare of the nation manifests itself in a free-market economy that functions within a democratic federation of states whose primary responsibility is to provide for the welfare of its citizens and to protect the country from foreign dangers. We also indicate that this philosophy generates a culture in which citizens enjoy many freedoms, including those of religion, speech, and press. We add that this philosophy has resulted in universal education as a way of preparing citizens to handle the responsibilities inherent in having so much freedom.

For purposes of comparison, we have students read excerpts from Marx and Engel's *The Communist Manifesto,* identify the values reflected in this document, and determine the effect of these values on economics, government, and culture. Students have no difficulty, after discussing the American documents, recogniz-ing the value placed by communism on the collective good to rid itself of the inequities it sees in a class-dominated capitalistic society.

Once students have considered these philosophies and the way they reflect the values of the societies, they are ready to develop philosophies based on the values they have bought. After students spend one class period working on their philosophies, we show the film *1984* in its entirety. With the cooperation of other teachers and the permission of the administration, we preempt three 45-minute class periods on the viewing day. This arrangement gives us the opportunity to show the film and discuss it on the same day. The goal of our discussion is to enable students to see the relationship between the values inherent in the philosophy of the society and its culture.

The analysis of the film assists students as they seek to complete the formulation of the philosophies for their societies. The following is characteristic of the kinds of statements students have developed:

> We hold these truths to be self-evident, that all persons have the right to live in perpetual peace and harmony. We believe this peace is nurtured by the values of honesty, love, and family. We also believe this peace results in universal happiness and mutual trust. The environment of peace enables all citizens to succeed in attaining the wealth they desire for a fulfilling life.

Next we ask each group to name its society, determine its geography and climate, create a map, design a flag, and write a national anthem that reflects the values of that society. With these activities, less academic students are successful because the tasks are concrete. This built-in success sustains interest in the total project.

As our students begin their projects, we remind them to keep in mind the values upon which they are basing their societies. We give them ample class time to work together on this project.

At this point we assign another component of the project. Because students are very much involved by this time and have considerable material upon which to base a written report, they will not be intimidated by this assignment. The students are asked to provide—in addition to the philosophy, the map and geographic description, the flag, and the anthem—a written description of the society's economy, government, and culture. The assignment also includes a section explaining how each value bought by the group has determined the nature of the society, leading to a consideration of what a day in the life of an average citizen of that society would be like. Each member of the group takes responsibility for completing one part of the group project.

When the projects are complete (we allow a week for the writing), students present their work to the class. We hang the flags and display the maps, sing the anthems, and videotape the presentations. Students respond enthusiastically to the work of their classmates and have a good time. Often we invite the principal and other administrators to attend the presentations. Excerpts from one of the projects follow.

Oren included a day in the life of a citizen in his group's presentation of the mythical society Pache:

> A typical day on Pache Island is not like the average American day. There aren't the same pressures and hardships that people here have to deal with. A person who is a senior in high school is treated as an adult. In most cases, this is the last year of their formal education. By this time they know what they will do with their lives. Every day families make sure they have a certain amount of time to spend together. Family is important to everyone. Each day family members talk about their little worries and help each

other work out their problems. Therefore, the day always ends positively. No one holds grudges. At night, there is no need to lock doors or windows because of the mutual trust of everyone on the island. Crime is nonexistent. Everyone loves one another, so there is little of the every day conflicts that we are so accustomed to. A typical day is peaceful, happy and satisfying.

Jack composed the national anthem for Pache to the tune of "My Country, 'Tis of Thee":

This island that you see
Is a loving family
Our Land of peace.

Land of trust and health and peace
Joy and even wealth for all
No place on earth we'd rather be
Our Island Home.

Anyone can join us here
There is no need for fear
On Pache's Shore

Someday the World will see
How easy peace can be
For any creed or race of man
Happy Isle of Peace.

Another group of students created the society of Sephald. They included a statement of philosophy reflecting the values of their country:

We hold these truths to be self-evident, that all persons are born with several unalienable rights. Among these are love, hope, and the pursuit of success as defined by each citizen. The people are guaranteed privacy, but people shall cooperate with each other in times of need. These rights are a source of pride to the people who enjoy excitement and love in Sephald.

Jen described education in Sephald:

Education is very important in Sephald. The system is different from that of the United States. In Sephald, all students must complete at least sixteen years of school, beginning at age four. Students may consider continuing their chosen path to success by attending a four year or eight year university after that.

This may sound stressful to the students, but the environment inside the schools provides a comfortable and exciting atmosphere. For example, dependability is encouraged through support groups. At the end of each school week, groups of ten students get together and talk about how the week has gone. If they have any problems, they are able to find help from peers. Although open discussion is encouraged in these meetings, the privacy of each individual is highly respected.

Sephald's students become close to their teachers, mainly because the faculty to student ratio is 1:4. Students really get to know their teachers almost as if they were family. The teachers are very kind to the students, using only positive reinforcement in all situations. Students are encouraged to be proud of what they do and to always be hopeful. With the help of close friends and caring teachers, there is a constant feeling of love in all classrooms, which enables all students to succeed.

After the students complete their presentations, we ask them to reflect on the work in their journals, considering such questions as: "How difficult was it to select your values? What were some of the problems you faced in constructing your society? What did you learn about the importance of values in determining the nature of a society?"

Now that the students are completely engaged and feeling confident in their ability to succeed in our course, we are ready to introduce some demanding individual assignments. We want students to begin to take responsibility for their own learning. To begin this process, we introduce *When the Legends Die* by Hal Borland (Bantam, 1984).

We ask students to write a journal in which they imagine themselves being put in a society where they are unable to live by the values important to them. In discussing the journal entries, we talk about how they would react and feel in such a situation, how this experience would affect them as people. Then we tell them that *When the Legends Die* is about a Native American, a Ute, who is forced to abandon his own customs and live in the white man's world. We read the first chapter aloud, focusing on the mother, Bessie, from whose perspective this part of the story is told. Students continue reading through to the end of Book I.

Based on their reading, students work together in small groups to identify Ute values: the singing of songs to celebrate all aspects of life, the oneness of all life (hence, the round house), the choosing by the individual of his own name, killing animals only out of necessity, and the sharing of food with their animal brothers. Each student is then asked to write a persona journal from the viewpoint of Bessie that describes what happened to her and her family as a result of contact with the white man's world. In these journals they talk about her experiences with Blue Elk, who betrayed his people for money, the death of her husband, and her commitment to teaching her son the Ute traditions that will enable him to survive with pride and dignity.

Students then read Book II, in which the boy, who has named himself Bear's Brother, is wrenched from his independent life and forced to adopt the white man's values. Students are asked to write persona journals as Bear's Brother telling what happened after Bessie died. They share their journals, which reveal their frustration and anger at having to abandon all that was important in their lives.

Next, we write the following quotation on the board:

> "Go away," the boy said [to the bear]. "Go, or they will kill you. They do not need guns to kill. They kill without guns. Listen! I speak truth. They will kill you. Go away!" (p. 73)

Students explain in their journals the significance to the boy of these words. As they share their latest journal entries, we begin to refer to the boy as Tom. If the students don't pick up on this shift, we call their attention to the signif-icance of the name change as indicative of his forced acceptance of the white man's world. We discuss the relationship of a person's name to his or her conception of self. We remind students of the meanings of their names and ask how they would feel if they were forced to adopt a new name. Even though some students say they wouldn't mind changing their name, most couldn't imagine having a different name. One student said, "I wouldn't be me if I had a different name." For a follow-up journal entry, we ask students to predict the effect on Tom of this name change.

Students then read Book III, in which Tom Black Bull becomes the notorious Killer Tom Black, the most vicious rider in the rodeo circuit. We discuss Tom's relationship with Red Dillon, focusing on what might make Tom so angry with the world. (Red does not let Tom win and uses him to make money dishonorably.) In a persona journal, as Killer Tom, students describe the anger that led to the destruction of Red's house after Meo's death. In sharing these journals, we lead students to see that Tom's anger is a secondary emotion. He's frustrated and in despair, feeling he has no real identity. This frustration leads to the anger. We take this opportunity to extend the discussion to our own lives in order to help students understand what generates their own feelings of anger. Sometimes this discussion can last an entire class period, but we think it is worth it because the story helps students gain insight into themselves and their emotional lives.

Students complete the novel with the reading of Book IV. We ask them to write down at least five questions they have about Tom's actions in this section. Invariably students wonder why he ran away from Nurse Redmond, why he went back to the mountains, why he didn't kill the bear, and why he decided to stay in the mountains. These and other questions generate lively discussion, even arguments about the wisdom of his ultimate decision to return to the old ways. To prompt students to find answers to these questions for themselves based on their review of the text, we ask them to assume the persona of Tom (once again Bear's Brother) to explain his reasons for returning to the mountain. In so doing, we tell them, they will also be explaining the meaning of the epigraph, "When the legends die, the dreams end. When the dreams end, there is no more greatness." Danielle's paper reflects the careful attention our students give to this assignment.

> Why did I come back to the mountain? Because I saw a bear, a grizzly and got the idea that I had to kill it. But why? Because I am killer Tom Black and I want to forget that I am a Ute, that's why!
> I woke this morning after having a restless night filled with bad dreams, mostly about my mother and the old tales I refuse to remember. The brush

by the creek bank was dripping, but the air was clear and crisp as always after a rain. A few degrees lower and it would have been frosty. This reminded me of mornings at the lodge my father had built, when my mother sang at her work and taught me little songs about yellow leaves, greedy squirrels, and fawns that had lost their spots.

Later in the morning I walked to a place where I could look off to the southeast and see Horse Mountain. That brought back the bitter memory of another frosty morning, when I discovered the burnt ruins of the lodge, and meeting Benny Grayback and the old man called Fish, waiting at the foot of Horse Mountain to take me back to the school.

I pushed that memory behind me and continued walking. Then I came across wet muddy bear tracks. The trail wandered, zigzagging back up the mountain, doubling back on itself. There was no doubt in my mind that the bear tracks were made by a grizzly. I worked my way along the trail to a place near a small creek, and began to build a makeshift lodge.

By afternoon I was able to lay out a line to follow the bear. I forced myself to stop thinking like a man and begin to think like a bear. I followed the line, then I hid behind a rock, and drifted to sleep. When I awoke, there was something just beyond me surrounded by light. It was a woman. I could not see her features, but something inside of me knew who she was. She was the All-Mother, the mothers and grandmothers all the way back to the beginning.

I began chanting. I was singing the bear chant. I closed my eyes, and when I opened them she was gone, but I saw the bear. As I tried to shoot I closed my eyes, fighting with myself. "I came to kill the bear! To be myself!"

Then something made me realize that the bear had not made trouble. The trouble was in me. And I put my rifle down without shooting. I heard the All-Mother singing the star chant.

Knowing what I must do, I stripped myself naked and went to the creek. I stepped in and began to bathe. Then naked and unarmed, I started up the mountain. As I traveled, I began to notice the roundness of everything. The sun, the path it follows, the blue roundness of the sky and the aspen trunks. When I stopped to rest, I closed my eyes and sang a song to the roundness of everything. I drifted off to sleep. Dreams came. First unwanted dreams. I was in a corral at the agency and I was riding a huge frosty bear. It lunged from the chute and I lashed at it and raked it with my spurs. It lunged three more times. But now it was no longer a bear but a bronc, the big roan bronc. It fell and I was trapped in the saddle. But I crawled free and stood up, and there was Red Dillon saying, "You double-cross me and I'll break your goddam neck!" I struck Red Dillon with my fist and he was gone. A horse was struggling on the ground, a big black bronc. It lifted its head, snorted bloody foam and then fell back with a thud, and died.

Then I dreamed I was a boy, lost and crying in my loneliness beside the cold char of the lodge. Then the lodge was gone and I was sitting in the night, watching the flames go into the sky. I was at the hospital and Mary

Redmond was saying, "Put away your tomahawk and take the feathers out of your hair." I dreamed I was alone, walking over the earth in the night. I came to a mountain and said, " I have forgotten who I am." There was no answer. I continued, "I was a boy who went with Blue Elk and did what he said I must do." Still no answer. "I killed as they taught me to kill." The mountain answered, "Why?" And I answered, "I had to kill the past. I had to be myself. And now there is nothing left to kill except myself for I did not kill the bear."

When I woke, I saw white all around me, the light of truth and understanding. I sat thinking what had driven me to hunt the bear in the first place. I reached back to the beginning and began to hunt down all the painful things of my past to kill them. All except the bear, my childhood, and my heritage, all that I had tried to kill when I became Killer Tom Black. When I was younger, my mother told me, "When you are a man you will have a tail, though you will never see it, you will always have something behind you." Now I understand. Time lays scars like the chipmunks stripes, paths that lead from where he is now back to where he came from, from the eyes of his knowing to the tail of his remembering. They are ties that bind a man to his own being, his small part of the roundness. Now I know I am bound to my heritage and I have made peace with myself. And now I understand that "when the legends die, the dream ends. When the dream ends there is no more greatness."

After several days of reading, discussing, and writing, we change the pace by preparing students to create a "shield" for Tom Black Bull (see page 14). With the class, we identify the major colors that are used symbolically throughout the book: red for protection; blue for security; black for manliness; white for wholeness; and yellow for life. Working in pairs, students find specific references to these colors. We help them by indicating the chapters, sometimes even the exact pages. If they don't mention the paradoxical use of red and blue with Red Dillon and Blue Elk, we point that out to them. This also provides a review of the entire book, culminating in the creation of the shield.

We distribute a circular shield to represent wholeness, with four feathers hanging from different points around the periphery. Students are instructed to draw the animal that represents Tom in the center space. In each of the four quadrants, students are to represent pictorially the symbolism inherent in the color imagery. For example, red represents protection. In the story, Bessie buys Tom a red blanket, and later Mary Redmond, the red-headed nurse, offers Tom her protection. Students might represent red symbolically by drawing a red blanket in one of the quadrants. In a like manner they complete the other sections of the shield by finding representations for the meanings of blue, white, and yellow. Because black represents maleness, students will probably find it the appropriate color for the bear. Students are instructed to write on the feathers the four dominant values in Tom's life as a Ute, such as truth, the oneness of all life, tradition, and self-respect.

After students have completed the shield for Tom Black Bull, we ask them to create a personal shield so that we can return the focus to self-exploration.

Students create their shields in the same way they made Tom's shield. To get them started, we send them back to their journals to review the descriptions of their values and tell them not to use words but to rely on pictorial representation and color to reflect themselves and their values. For example, one section of the shield might depict something about themselves they take pride in, such as being named to the JV football team, having paid for a new car, or having made the honor roll. Students complete the other quadrants accordingly. For the center they select an animal that best reflects their personality. On each of the feathers they write one of their important values.

As a culminating activity, students complete a "Who Am I?" project. The format for this project should be presented to them early. It is divided into three sections: (1) Who am I now? (2) Who was I? (their background); and (3) Who am I becoming? They have a head start on the first section because they have already explored their values in several of the preceding exercises. In journal entries they can now rank-order *all* of the values from the values auction from most to least important and justify their first and last selections. Now they examine their interests, hobbies, things they like, and things they dislike. This section can be written as a homework assignment.

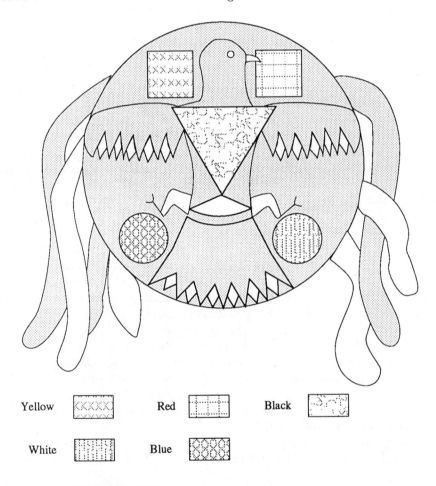

Yellow ⬚ Red ⬚ Black ⬚

White ⬚ Blue ⬚

Next the students examine the qualities that define them and write down the most important of these in their journals. To make this easier, students work with a partner, preferably someone who knows them well.

After class brainstorming of possible qualities to be included, each partner describes her or his idea of the qualities that define the other. In addition to being an engaging activity, it is also an enlightening one. We often aren't really conscious of how others view us. Students exchange journals and respond to their accuracy or lack of it by writing a note in the partner's journal. They then copy the information from the partner in their own journals and use it as the basis for discussion of the qualities that they believe most clearly describe themselves. We encourage them to include specific things that they have done that reflect these qualities, and something about the meaning of their names.

At this point, if the class is willing, students can share these self-revelations. Otherwise we collect journals and comment briefly on the progress to date, reassuring students that in this prewriting phase all that matters is the information gathered and not the form or presentation of the material.

Once the journals have been returned to the students, they move on to the next stage of information gathering for the "Who am I now?" section. They should refer to the journal entry that began this unit: an experience that affected their lives. After rereading that entry, they write about whether they have changed recently—and if so, how and why.

By now students have enough material to write the first section of their paper. We may elect to stop at this point and encourage them to refine what they have already written, or we may choose to continue the journal writing and ask them to explore the information needed for the second section of the report: the "Who was I?" (background) section. Some of the areas that can be explored include the effects of family and tradition on the individual; customs and rituals in their families; the effects of friends; the effects of places they have been; the town, city, or country they were raised in and the effects of that on shaping them; their brothers and sisters and their effects; the effects of religion or the absence of religion on their lives; and the effects of specific experiences they have had. In each case students will need guidance to ensure that they don't just list the categories but get involved in very specific and personal ways in discussing the significance of each one.

Again, depending upon the needs and makeup of the class, it may be best to stop here and let the students concentrate on developing this section more fully and formally. Otherwise they can move on to a consideration of the "Who am I becoming?" section—their future. They should examine their short- and long-range goals. What are they planning for the summer, for next year, for after high school? In addition, they should discuss their career goals, if any, and the reasons for their choice. Also of interest are their plans for marriage and children. An interesting addendum is to ask them to reflect on the life they think they'll be leading 10 years from now and describe it in as much detail as they can.

Now they are ready to draft the entire report. Because so much thinking and writing have already taken place, it is primarily a revising and rewriting activity. To facilitate this phase in the process, we encourage them to use word processors for composing their final papers.

Alicia, wrote the following as her "Who Am I?" project:

> Writing about myself was not as easy as I thought it would be. It's funny how little time we spend on thinking about what it is that makes each of us tick. I had to think hard and long before I could put into words a description of who I am and what factors contributed to my being who I am. Something struck me as odd, as I thought of the real me. Had I been asked to write about myself just two years ago, the description would have been totally different. I sometimes feel that my life began just two years ago. It is easy to forget pain and very difficult to recall it. But I would be cheating the reader, as well as myself, if I did not include some mention of my first twelve years of life. I suppose some of the ways I view things today have a lot to do with my past. I hope I do myself some justice in reviewing my past, my present and my future.
>
> I'm a typical teenager, sixteen years old, healthy, active and probably a royal pain to my parents. My values have changed quite a lot in the past few years. I now greatly value the rights of women and other minorities. I value my freedom of speech and the right to choose to become whatever I desire. I value the right of women to choose their own destinies and to choose what is best for their bodies.
>
> I'm interested in typical teenager things. I love dancing, socializing with my friends and I love boys, especially older, good looking ones. I love photography, an art form inspired by a former teacher, and hope to pursue a career in that field. I guess I could become a dancing photographer or cinematographer and die happy.

She then goes on to describe some personal details of a difficult childhood. In the final section, she writes:

> I look upon my mother now as a courageous human being, who overcame many obstacles and was able to deliver us from the gates of hell. My aunt, whom I consider my other parent, is another example of a strong, courageous woman who has not allowed others to use her gender as a means of stopping her from succeeding in life. I have great respect for all women who fight the odds in order to succeed.
>
> My goals are many. For the near future, I hope to succeed in school and be able to go on to college. I would like to major in the arts, specializing in cinematography. I would like to travel someday, doing camera work for a film company. Most importantly, I would like to become the kind of woman who will stand up for her rights and the rights of others, who is strong of character and values. I would like to someday have a family and children of my own, and be able to instill in them the same values taught to me by my mom and my aunt.

"This Is Your Life" breaks through the shell that disenchanted students have constructed to protect them from the feelings of "nobodiness" described by Emily Dickinson in her poem. However unlike Dickinson's playful notion that to be somebody is dreary, we want our students to enjoy the recognition their successful mastery of the reading and writing in this unit affords them.

Addendum

When more than one or two students have given names such as Lakesha, Quinzell, Ju'Von, Ping-lin, and the like, we replace the Name Game with Star Search. In this case we prepare by learning the birth date of each student and thus his or her astrological sign.

On the first day of class, instead of telling students what their names mean, we tell them what their astrological signs are, though they usually know, and, accordingly, what personal characteristics they supposedly possess. *Astrology*, by Roy A. Gallant (Doubleday, 1974) or *Larousse Encyclopedia of Astrology*, edited by Jean-Louis Brall, Helen Weaver and Allan Edwards (McGraw-Hill Book Co., 1977), provide concise descriptions of people born under each of the 12 signs of the zodiac.

These revelations generate the same classroom banter as the Name Game does. And, as with the name meanings, we instruct our students to jot down what they learn about their individual star sign, assuring them they will need this information later. Sometimes we have distributed printed copies of each student's star sign description, but usually we don't do that because we want students to listen and take notes.

Once students have taken notes about their star signs, we ask them to write us a letter about how well the star sign descriptions characterize them. We expect them to go into some detail as they accept or reject the astrological descriptions of their personalities.

From here on, the procedures are the same as the Name Game (see page 1).

Some other Works that can be used in this unit

Achebe, Chinua. *Things Fall Apart.* 1959. New York: Fawcett Crest, 1985.

Angelou, Maya. *I Know Why the Caged Bird Sings.* 1970. New York: Bantam, 1983.

Borland, Hal. *When the Legends Die.* New York: Bantam, 1984.

Cisneros, Sandra. *The House on Mango Street.* New York: Random House, 1989.

Fast, Howard. *April Morning.* 1961. New York: Bantam, 1983.

Myers, Walter Dean. *Fallen Angels.* New York: Scholastic, 1988.

Orwell, George. *Animal Farm.* 1946. New York: NAL Signet Classics, 1986.

—————. *1984.* 1949. New York: NAL, 1983.

Parks, Gordon. *The Learning Tree.* New York: Fawcett Crest, 1987.

Wiesel, Eli. *Night.* New York: Bantam, 1982.

BLUE HIGHWAYS

> *On the old highway maps of America, the main routes were red and the back roads blue. Now even the colors are changing, but in those brevities just before dawn and a little after dusk—times neither day nor night—the old roads return to the sky some of its color. Then, in truth, they carry a mysterious cast of blue and it's that time when the pull of the blue highway is strongest, when the open road is beckoning, a strangeness, a place where a man can lose himself.*
>
> William Least Heat Moon

In his book Blue Highways, William Least Heat Moon describes his travels along the back roads of the United States. His appealing narrative inspired us to pull out a road map to find those blue highways in our own community. What we discovered, not surprisingly, is that these out-of-the-way places have nothing apparently noteworthy about them at first glance. But it's on these ordinary, unpretentious roads that most of us live and work. That's when we realized that, in a symbolic sense, most of us live our lives on blue highways.

However, it is this very ordinariness that fascinates Least Heat Moon and in which he sees vitality and drama. To appreciate the value of life around us is a primary goal of this unit. Rather than seeing our homely surroundings and daily life as boring, we can discover the exciting and even the extraordinary if we learn how to look for them.

Because of our students' inherent fascination with the concept of their local "blue highways," it is easy for us as English teachers to engage their interest to teach the reading, writing, speaking, and listening skills they need to learn.

To engage the students, we purchase from local gasoline stations maps of our town and surrounding areas. We ask the students to find their town, their school, their street or road, where they work, and their local hangouts. We ask them to see how many of the important places of their daily lives are on blue highways, as opposed to main thoroughfares. We have them mark these significant locations with their initials.

Now we introduce the book Blue Highways and display a large map of the United States. We tell them that they will be reading excerpts from the book. Fortunately it is the kind of book that lends itself to the reading of excerpts. We tell them that Least Heat Moon traveled around the country—and it literally was around the country—following the blue highways. (As we name the places he visited, we indicate in general where they are on the map.) He didn't visit places most people have heard of. For example, when he went to Texas, he skipped

Dallas and went to Dime Box instead. In California, he avoided Los Angeles and San Francisco in favor of Hat Creek. In Montana he visited Shelby, which we had trouble finding, and in New Jersey he visited Othello. In all these places, he writes about ordinary people living unremarkable—but to him fascinating—lives.

We ask the students where in the United States they would like to visit. They might only be able to name a state or a general geographic area. Based on their responses, we assign different parts of the book, not worrying about the entire book being covered, much less each student reading the entire book. We put them in groups of four, making sure that at least one student in the group is a strong reader. We have one student at a time read a section aloud while the other group members listen. Then they discuss it, looking for interesting and humorous details. One student acts as recorder for the group. We suggest 20 minutes for reading and note taking in small groups. We allow the rest of the period for each group to share with the class the results of their reading.

This procedure is time consuming, but for disenchanted students the support of the small group performing a specific, limited task adds interest, limits the individual risk, and builds in opportunities for success. We allow only a few periods for this reading activity, long enough for them to get a feel for Least Heat Moon's book. Also, we ask students to jot down noteworthy details.

Next we have each reading group make a map of the school, inside and outside, indicating the "blue highways" and the main thoroughfares. When we share the maps, we find that not everyone agrees as to which corridors are main thoroughfares and which inside and outside areas are blue highways. This is all right because disagreement generates interest and extends the definition of a blue highway. We are now able to get the students to think symbolically and metaphorically about the concept of blue highways. In one class after this discussion a student remarked that he thought he was a blue highways person. Obviously, he had seen the metaphorical significance of this idea.

A logical extension of this assignment is to introduce the idea of each student recording her or his experiences on the blue highways of the school in the same way Least Heat Moon recorded the everyday experiences on the blue highways of his travels. Students may need help getting started on this assignment, so we ask them to jot down what they see from wherever they are in the classroom. We tell them what we see from where we are sitting or standing. For example, "Chris has a huge earring shaped like a cross in his left ear. He wears a black leather jacket and a heavy-metal tee shirt. He plays around on his desk with his tapes and headset, temporarily disengaged from his head."

What students see depends on where they are sitting and what details they find interesting or noteworthy. We give them some time to do this and then encourage sharing with the class or with a partner. Then we ask them to try to remember something they heard during the period and to write it down. We share these observations. The purpose of this exercise is to give students experience in seeing, listening, and recording details from their own experiences. At the same time, we build their confidence that this is a task they can complete successfully.

We tell the students that they will keep a journal of their experiences in the school. For some students it may be best for us to keep the journals in the classroom. We arrange with the administration of the school for permission to send the students into the various parts of the campus to make observations for their journals. Our students are released for most of the period, allowing time for them to return to the classroom, make a brief report to us on their activities, and turn in their journals. Students might follow this same procedure two days in a row. Then they share their entries with the students in their groups. Chris wrote the following after a visit to the "wall," the school smoking area:

"Give me a butt, Carlos!" demanded Gary, a tall, dark haired boy leaning against the fence of the smoking area that separates the "wall" from the high school football and soccer fields.

Carlos dug deep into his pocket and pulled out a half worn pack of Lucky Strikes. He picked one out for Gary and another for himself.

"Yeah, well, these are my last butts," Carlos said, crumbling the pack and throwing it over his shoulder.

"Do ya have a light to go along with it?" Gary asked.

"You're really pushing it," said Carlos .

Gary looked up with a half grin on his face. His eyes were trying to peer through the long hair in front of them to see what Carlos would do.

"Well, get your light out already, dude," Carlos said impatiently.

Gary whipped out his Zippo and with a flick of his thumb lit both cigarettes with a five inch flame.

"Don't get so close to my hair, man," Carlos warned.

"Just shut up and finish your butt," Gary responded. Both boys leaned against the wall, finishing their butts, soaking up the sunshine and watching two girls who had just come outside.

After two days of traveling on their own blue highways, our students are told to read about Least Heat Moon's travels to Dime Box, Texas (page 138) or to Nameless, Tennessee (page 29). We read sections of these chapters aloud, noting the frequency and richness of dialogue and pointing out the punctuation. We ask students to note the paragraphing of dialogue and the placement of various punctuation marks—in short, we are teaching the graphics of grammar. We ask them to select one of their journal entries that has dialogue in it or, if it does not, to invent some dialogue (for this, they are invited to solicit help from a group member) and punctuate it as Least Heat Moon does.

The next assignment is to go back to their blue highways and listen for and record what people say, returning to the class before the end of the period. The next day they share what they have recorded with their small groups, and using Least Heat Moon's visit to Dime Box as a model, they revise and rewrite their latest observations. This revision and rewriting process may take another period. We encourage students to share their entries with the whole class. Kris reported on her observations of the high school food service cashier:

■ Even early in the morning the cafeteria is filled with a lot of noise, activity, and aromas. But there is also something I always look forward to, and this is seeing Vera, that's what all the kids call her, the cafeteria cashier. She is the sweetest lady in the school and has this almost magical way to cheer you up.

"Good morning, sweetie pie. How are ya'?" Vera greets me as I walk in the café.

"Fine, Vera. How are you?" I reply, still somewhat sleepy.

"Okay, dollface, what will you have? Just coffee?" Vera asks in her motherly way.

"Yes, Vera, that's it. I really don't have time to eat." I hand her fifty cents.

"Yo, Vera, where's the rolls?" a tall boy screams across the line.

"Hold on, honey. Can't you see I'm helping someone else?" Vera says.

No matter how nasty or aggressive the kids get with her, Vera is always her sweet self. She rarely ever yells, and if she does, she still puts a "honey" or a "sweetie" with it.

By now kids are piling in and out of the cafeteria fast. The first bell rings, and everybody runs.

"Well, I don't got twenty cents!" a boy tells Vera.

"You need twenty cents to buy that, dollie," Vera explains.

"But what am I goin' to eat? C'mon, I'll pay ya back," the boy pleads.

After a few more arguments, Vera gives in like she usually does. She doesn't want to see anyone go hungry.

"Okay, honey, go ahead, but remember, you owe me," Vera says, trying to sound stern, but also knowing she is probably never going to see that money again.

Tracy wrote this after a visit to the school's "greaser cafeteria."

■ "Hey Richie, let me see your box, I want to listen to a tape I have," says Tom.

"No. The batteries are going dead," Richie tells him.

"I won't play it loud, come on, don't be a jerk."

"Okay, but don't play it loud," replies Richie. Tom pops the cassette into the box and the loud thrashing music of Metallica starts to play.

"Yo, Tom, turn it up man," yells Will from across the table.

Marc starts tapping his hands to the sporadic beat of the music. Tom turns the radio up as the next song begins to play. This gets the attention of the lunch lady.

"Hey, turn that thing off!" she yells in her crone-like voice.

"Hey? There's nobody here named Hey," replies Tom.

He turns to Will. "Is your name Hey?"

"Nope, nobody here named Hey," says Will.

"Don't be a wise guy," retorts the lunch lady.

Ignoring her last comment, Tom asks, "Is your name Hey?"

"Hey," yells the lunch table crowd. "Hey!"

"So," Tom continues, "is your name Hey?"

"Could be, could be," replies the lunch lady.

"Oh, so now your name is B," comments Will. "I wish you would make up your mind." Another round of "Hey's" is bellowed by the table crowd. The lunch lady walks out of the cafeteria. She returns with a smirk on her face and a pudgy man nobody recognizes. The pudgy man leans against the wall, as if he thinks his presence will deter Tom and the rowdy group. Of course he is wrong.

"Who the hell is that guy?" demands Tom.

"He's the new narc," replies Elaine.

"Yeah, he gets paid to walk around the halls and spy on us," explains Carrie.

"He looks like he's pregnant," says Will.

"He couldn't have been a cop. He's too fat," comments Tom who turns the music up louder as the "narc" approaches the table.

"Turn that off!" he orders.

"I can't, it's broken, it won't turn off," Tom says.

"If you want to keep it, then turn it off!"

Richie reaches across the table and turns off the radio. The narc abruptly walks back to his wall.

"Yo, it's too quiet in here," comments Mike.

"That guy is a real jerk," Tom says, still mulling over the episode with the radio.

As a culminating activity for this introduction to the unit, students select their best entries for inclusion in the class's own Blue Highways. For this revising and rewriting activity, we encourage the use of computer word-processing programs. Students are far more willing to revise and correct their work on a computer than revise work done by hand. Besides, they take pride in the perfectly printed finished products that will form the text for the class book. Tracy, who wrote the cafeteria observations, organized her notes on the computer and conferred with another student and the teacher for help on punctuating the dialogue and controlling the verb tenses. Then, seeing how frequently she had used *says*, asked another student for suggestions of alternative verbs. Because she didn't know how to spell some of the words she wanted to use, we told her not to worry about spelling while she was drafting and revising, that when she finished writing she could use the computer's spelling checker to make any necessary corrections. As a result, Tracy felt free to experiment with diction, a freedom she had not had before. Without the computer, Tracy admitted, she would have been much less motivated, to revise, edit, and correct with so much care.

Often we use the Blue Highways project as the basis for a character sketch or short story. When we do, some students need to focus more attention on real characters or situations. Because most of our students spend several hours a day at their part-time jobs, we encourage them to become observers and recorders of what they see and hear where they work. Jason developed a journal fragment of what happened to him at his job in a fast-food restaurant into this piece:

The chairs and tables that filled the restaurant were still empty, but it was early. I turned the corner and went behind the counter into the kitchen.

"Que pasa, amigo." Jose called from across the store, a dopey looking grin on his face. I knew it was going to be a bad day because already at 8 o'clock in the morning his voice was annoying. I half-heartedly returned the greeting.

"Jason. Where's your hat?" the restaurant manager yelled from her office.

"I, um, forgot it."

"AGAIN! That's the third time this week. What the hell are you going to wear?"

"Don't worry about it." I put on a fake smile to try to joke my way out of it, but by the look in her eyes I knew that it wasn't going to work.

"No, I'm going to worry about it." Liz looked around her office, picked something up then turned back to me.

"Here, wear this." She tossed me a large pink and orange crown with the words BURGER KING printed on it in large yellow letters. Reluctantly, I placed it on my head and went to the front of the store to punch in.

The breakfast hours were not busy and seemed to drag on for days. I kept adjusting the crown, which felt extremely heavy on my brow, in hopes of getting it to look somewhat decent. At about 10:30 (a half hour before breakfast ended), the door to the restaurant opened and in walked what had to be one of the most beautiful creatures I'd ever seen on this earth. She had long blond hair and a body that could cause anybody to look twice. She walked up to the counter and put on a smile that other girls would die for.

"Can I help you?" I said in the most flirtatious way I could.

"I'll just have a small Diet Coke," she replied in a voice that was hypnotizing to me.

I took her money and then went to the other end of the counter to get her drink, which she quietly waited for. When I handed her the cup she smiled at me, but it wasn't the gorgeous smile of before. It was a sarcastic smile.

"What are you supposed to be? The burger king?" This time her voice wasn't hypnotizing, but malicious. She turned and walked from the counter, and I knew she laughed to herself. I went to the bin of hashbrowns to get one and sulk. Jose was standing there with that dopey grin on his face.

"Muy bonita," he said pointing at the blond girl.

"Shut up," I said and walked away from him.

The lunch hour came and went quickly with only a few people commenting on my crown, but every one angered me more than the one before. I knew I couldn't take much more of it. As I leaned against one of the front counter registers, I kept thinking about the girl in the morning. I was interrupted when a man entered the restaurant. I recognized him from being at the drive-thru window minutes before. He walked up to the counter with a small bag of half eaten french fries in his hand.

"Are you the kid who took my order?" He was walking to me, but his eyes were focused to my left. I smelled alcohol on his breath.

"Yes, I am. Is there a problem?" I was being as polite as possible to the man.

"Damn right, there's a problem. I ordered french fries and there ain't no ketchup in the bag."

"You didn't ask . . ."

"I shouldn't hafta ask for nothin. I'm a white, paying customer."

At this point, Liz had been drawn to the front by his yells.

"When I come to a . . . aw hell, get me the manager. I don't want to talk to some kid in a stupid lookin' crown."

"That's it!" I yelled at the top of my lungs. I took the crown from the top of my head and threw it into the customer's face.

"I quit."

I left the store, never wanting to be the "burger king" again.

One of the writing skills our students need for success in most English classes—and certainly in social studies, science, and health classes—is the ability to write a research paper. To help them learn to write in a transactional mode, we use the expressive, informal writing of the Blue Highways activity as a way of engaging students in the process of ethnographic research, which becomes the basis for critical writing.

As a result of their Blue Highways research, students are more aware of the issues of real concern to students in the school. Some of these issues in our school have been the banning of headsets and boom boxes, the creation of smoking areas for students, student desire for an "open campus," the quality of cafeteria food and service, grading procedures, a districtwide ban on television viewing for one week, and hall passes. Of course the issues vary from year to year, but regardless of what the hot topics are, students determine the issues of greatest relevance to them.

In their journals they write their feelings about whatever issue they have chosen. Then we tell our students we want them to find out how others feel about these issues. To gather this information, they are going to interview three or four people most involved with or affected. However, before they begin their investigations, they need to know what kinds of questions to ask. We model the procedure by playing the obvious role of a teacher who wants to know how kids feel about the issue of, let's say, an open campus. We interview one or two students, asking, "How do you feel about having to remain at school throughout the day? Why do administrators object to students leaving and returning to the campus? How do teachers feel about this issue? What do parents think?" We tell our students that as they ask questions and get answers, other questions will probably come to them, especially questions about why students would want to leave the campus during the day.

Based on our example, students practice their interviewing techniques by questioning each other. We give them ample class time to interview three students, each from another issues group, and take notes on their interviews. We encourage students to ask "Why?" or "Tell me more" or "Give me an example" when they get one-word answers. As they work, we circulate, listening to their interviews, helping them elicit more information, and making suggestions for note taking.

After the first interview is completed, we stop the discussion process and tell our students to review their notes and expand on them, adding details they heard but didn't have time to write down. Once they have completed their in-class interviews and are feeling more comfortable with the process, they are ready to go out into the school to gather additional information from students, teachers, administrators, and other appropriate school personnel.

As students begin to assess the information they are collecting, they usually discover that as important as the data from the interview is, it's not enough to do justice to the full scope of the issues for a research paper. They may need to do library research, looking particularly for help from periodicals; to write or call other schools; or to get information from parents and others in the community. We help them with this part of their research by suggesting additional resources, making appointments with town officials, and showing them how to use the *Readers' Guide to Periodical Literature*, the microfiche catalog, and the public library computer network.

Michelle's paper reveals what she learned about television viewing from both her ethnographic and library research, as well as what she learned about citing her research sources using the MLA format.

Television has been an inseparable companion for most of America's youngsters since the early 1950's. Today, cable has vastly expanded the supply of programming. The VCR has turned favorite shows and movies into an endlessly repeatable pass-time[sic]. Video games have added to the home box's allure. (Tynan 75) When several elementary school kids were asked if they liked to act out their favorite characters, all responded yes. These characters ranged from Superman, Wonder Woman, She-ra, a Teenage Mutant Ninja Turtle, to some great looking man or woman.

But don't think TV is just for kids. Adults as well have fallen in love with TV. From my own experience, I see my father come home from work and plop down in front of the TV, and my older brother spends the entire day in front of the TV, he even sleeps there! The only time we have dinner as a family is on a holiday or when company is over. Jenn Curtis, a high school senior, says that she spends about four hours a day in front of the TV. This averages about 28 hours a week. She enjoys watching shows like "In Living Color," and "The Bundies." She admits to taking on the same attitude that her favorite character gives off. Jenn does about one hour of homework a night, and it is done in front of the TV. Dinner is eaten separately from the family, and in front of the TV also. Her mother often yells at her to turn it off, but she doesn't listen.

Jenn, my father and mother agree that television affects the family greatly. We don't communicate, and the time we do spend together is shortened if not lost altogether. In many families, the parents are unable to care for physically active kids, so they simply let the television occupy them. The television experience only reduces opportunities for children to work out basic family relationships, and thereby come to understand themselves better. Children also need to acquire fundamental skills in communication: to learn to read, write, and express themselves in order to function in everyday society. (Winn 60)

Michelle goes on to provide some data on nationwide TV viewing habits, citing her sources and providing appropriate quotes. She concludes her paper by recommending the proposed districtwide TV turn-off.

Kevin studied the issue of the open campus. His research led him to realize that the issue was more controversial than he had originally thought.

Should Yorktown High School have an open campus? That is the question many students, teachers, and administrators have asked themselves. Should students be allowed to come and go as they please during free periods?

Bernadette, a senior, believes that an open campus should be a privilege for seniors only. "Seniors are mature enough to leave and come back on time," she says, "and they are aware of the consequences if they don't." Laura, another senior, would like to see an open campus for all grades but only for those students who have earned the privilege through good behavior and good grades. She says it might actually "encourage students to go to class because they have more freedom."

Dr. Delaney, a math teacher, doesn't really see anything wrong with having an open campus for seniors as long as students have "decent academic records and no disciplinary problems." He remembers a time when our school had a semi-open campus. The students were allowed to roam the campus but not leave it. One student fell into the lake and sued the school. Ever since then, an open campus has been against school policy.

Our school principal strongly opposes the idea of an open campus. "If we allow students to come and go as they please, then we wouldn't know who leaves school in a car. There would be no control over the safety of those students." Because the school is responsible for the safety of all students, he was opposed to an open campus.

For many years the issue of an open campus at our school has been discussed. Always students have had a different attitude than teachers and administrators. Will there ever be an open campus at our school? Probably not.

Throughout the research process we reinforce what our students are discovering for themselves: that learning research skills is important not only for those who plan to go to college but for anyone who ever needs to know how to get information on any topic. Knowing how to access data from a variety of sources is a life skill that empowers us to find answers to many important questions about our world and ourselves, and to make informed decisions about what we believe and the actions we choose to take.

Like William Least Heat Moon, our students learn in this unit how to explore the highways of life and to appreciate the ordinary, everyday experiences of their lives. Equally important, they begin to appreciate themselves as a resource from which experience can be tapped as a springboard for learning about anything.

ADVICE AND CONSENSUS

Look to this day!
For it is life, the very life of life.
In its brief course lie all the varieties and realities of your existence:
The bliss of growth;
The glory of action;
The splendor of beauty;
For yesterday is already a dream, and tomorrow is only a vision;
But today, well lived, makes every yesterday
A dream of happiness, and every tomorrow a vision of hope.
Look well, therefore, to this day!
Such is the salutation of the dawn!

(Translated from the Sanskrit)

Something in our human nature motivates us to share our opinions and advise others. Just as the Indian poet counseled his friends to live for the day, to make the most of the moment, so do we; and our students frequently offer our advice to others. In fact, the writing of this book has been prompted by our desire to share with our colleagues what we have learned in our classrooms.

Our students also express their interest in each other 's welfare. In the halls between classes, in the cafeteria, in the classrooms before the bell rings, we hear bits and pieces of their conversations. Often they involve one student trying to counsel another. Sometimes these conversations are nothing more than mere gossip, but at other times they reveal a genuine concern for helping one another through the travails of adolescence. These conversations sometimes continue during class in the form of notes passed back and forth between students. Most teachers view these notes as an intrusion, diverting student interest from course work. Instead of paying attention to the day's lesson, students are preoccupied with personal concerns that generate some lively in–class correspondence. Rather than dismiss this activity as disruptive, we take advantage of our students' interest in communicating with each other to engage them in real-life experiences where students take responsibility for their own learning.

We begin by brainstorming on the concerns that might generate personal note writing. Our students identify boy-girl relationships, problems with parents, concerns about sex, drug use, and feelings of inferiority. They get very involved in sharing their concerns.

We ask students to select one problem area, identify a specific concern, and write a letter asking for advice. Sometimes students are self-conscious about writing on personal matters. If this is the case, we allow them to write the letters anonymously by assigning each student a number to identify himself or herself. Only after the exercise is completed do students reveal, if they choose, their authorship of the original letter.

The letters range from the very brief to quite long. For example, one student wrote:

I need to know how to help Mandy. She seems desperate and I am worried about her. Well, it all started when she was seeing this guy named Jim. It was last year around this time when they met at a teen night club. They liked each other very much and thought it would be cool to hang out and get to know each other better. So they did, and they started going out. Soon after, Mandy and Jim broke up. Mandy thought they would never have another chance, but Jim did not feel the same. Exactly one year later they met again and wanted to be together. They went places and had fun together. They talked on the phone all the time and really got along great. Then, all of a sudden, Mandy heard that Jimmy had another girlfriend as well. She was very upset. Why would he do this to her? She stopped speaking to him. Just last night, though, he called her and wanted to hang out again. She doesn 't know what to do. Will he hurt her again? She called me all upset and wanted my advice. I really was torn. Please help me to help her. What should I advise her to do?

Another wrote:

I need advice. My parents have decided to move to Florida. I really don't want to go. I don't want to leave my friends or my boyfriend, and I want to finish high school here. Nick said I could live with him until after my senior year. I really want to, but I 'm afraid my parents will be mad. What should I do?

Still another wrote:

Everyone thinks my family has no problems. It might seem that way, but my dad is an alcoholic. He has a job and everything, but once he gets home, he goes to the bottle. Last night, for instance, he really got out of hand, and I got scared he would hurt somebody. When he's tight, he blames me for everything. I ran away once, but I went back because I knew it wouldn't help him. I even called AA for him, but he refused to go. I have got to do something! I need help desperately.

Once students write these letters, they are very eager to receive letters in reply. To ensure a more meaningful response to the request for advice, we discuss in advance the kinds of information to include in such a letter. Our discussion resulted in the following general guidelines:

- Express understanding of the problem by restating it so the reader knows you are aware of the implications of the problem.
- If possible, connect the problem to some experience you know about or have experienced.
- Give complete advice, including several alternatives.
- Discuss each alternative with a scenario for what might happen.
- Conclude with a compassionate best wish.

For practice responding to a specific request for help on a problem, we give them the following request:

> I have been trying for years to get my sister to lose weight. It upsets me terribly to see her getting so fat, but I am at my wit's end. Nothing has seemed to work. She is up to 190 pounds and still growing. She is only 5 feet 3 inches. What can you suggest?

Each student responds to the request for help by creating a letter of advice. We share the responses, discussing how well each addressed the problem and adhered to the guidelines. One student wrote:

> I understand your problem very clearly because members of my family recently felt the same way about me. I knew I was overweight, but I could never have enough strength to admit that I knew it was a problem. It used to make me mad when someone in my family said I was fat. It took a lot of hard work and will–power, but I went on a diet and lost 31 pounds. What I'm trying to say is your sister has to do it for herself. If she doesn't accept that she has a problem, then it will just get worse. All you can do is be supportive. Good luck!

Another wrote:

> Well, I'm glad to see you are worried and upset by your sister's condition. Her weight problem could do damage to her health. Why not try and stop pressuring her for a while and see what happens? She might see that you have given up all hope and end up trying to show you up. Another thing you could do is suggest that she go to some type of weight loss program. For every 10 pounds she loses, offer her some type of gift. When I had to lose 35 pounds, I was given jewelry for every 10 pounds. Well, best of luck!

Students now respond to the original requests for help from their classmates. They are more eager than ever to see what their peers will say about their problems. About Mandy and Jim, one young man wrote:

> I think your friend Mandy is going to get herself in trouble if she sees this guy Jim. It's obvious that Jim is using her and likes playing games. I personally am going through the exact same situation with an ex-girlfriend of

mine. In this case, she claims she still loves me, and I still love her, but it's hard to go out again because of how she hurt me before.

I think Mandy should stay away from Jim and forget him. I mean, it's hard for me to give you good advice because I don't know if Jim really cares for her or not, but I think you should tell Mandy to be very careful. That's all I can tell you.

In response to the student whose parents were moving to Florida, one student wrote:

I understand your problem because I have one that is similar. There is one thing you have to think about. Who would you be happier with? If you can bear to spend every day with this person and his family and also follow the rules of that home, you're set. However, you can move to Florida and still keep in touch with your friends and your boyfriend. There are also other people in Florida that you can meet. Maybe you will meet someone just as special as your boyfriend.

Moving always seems like the worst thing to do, but it just may turn out better than you think. I think you'd be happier if you went with your parents. Whatever your decision, I'm sure your gonna make the best one!

In response to the student expressing concern about an alcoholic parent, one student wrote:

I can understand your problem. In my family, I have two alcoholic brothers. It is a very big problem. We had them go to AA. They did not refuse. In your case, your father refuses to go, but keep trying. Sit him down when he is sober and talk to him. Tell him he is ruining himself and his family; this might wake him up to what he is doing. Have the rest of your family give him a lot of support and help to try to kick the addiction of drinking. I hope you succeed.

These activities generate a great deal of student involvement as well as three pieces of writing: the request for advice, the letter to the sister of the overweight girl, and the replies to their classmates' requests for advice. In this exercise students also gain some experience with problem solving. Moreover, students write for real audiences, considering voice and tone as they compose their responses.

From here we move into literature activities, still using the device of letters of advice. Often in the literature we consider, protagonists confront problems similar to the ones students have dealt with in their personal correspondence. Students are asked to read a portion of a story or novel and give some advice to one of the characters. This activity promotes critical thinking and motivates students to finish reading the story to find out what happens. For example, after reading the section of *Inherit the Wind* in which Rachel asks Bertram Cates to retract his heresy against the Bible and put a stop to the trial, students are given the following letter:

Dear _____ :

I have a problem. I am on trial for breaking a law forbidding the teaching of evolution. I can lose my job. My girl threatens to leave me unless I recant. I am in turmoil. What should I do?

Sincerely,
Bertram Cates

In response to this question, several of our students wrote:

If I were you, I would not back down. There must have been a reason for you to go against the law in the first place. You should always fight for what you believe in. You are a teacher and you are supposed to help open their minds. You are only giving them a choice of what to believe. Before you came along, the children were forced to believe that man was created in seven days because that was the only thing they had. You have given the children something to think about. They now have a choice of what to believe.

Michele

I am very sorry about your predicament. It is a very serious one. You could recant to save yourself and your girl, but that would be turning your back on everything you believe. You think that kids have the right to know all aspects of biology including evolution, even though it seems to be against religious beliefs. If this is what you really believe, then backing down is the worst thing you can do. You should stand up for what you believe in and if your girlfriend doesn't understand, then that's her problem.

Eileen

You have a very big problem on your hands. I understand your concern about your welfare as well as your need to keep your girlfriend. But the best advice I have for you is to stick to your beliefs. If you back down now, you are indicating you were wrong in the first place. Though I know your love for your girlfriend is true, if she truly loves you as much as she says she does, she will stick by you. Stick to what you believe no matter what the risks.

Debbie

I really sympathize with your situation because I am a strong believer in free speech and free expression. I have but one suggestion for you. You are teaching evolution as if it is the absolute truth. Why not make a concession to the "good folk" of the town and teach both theories as different possible explanations. I wish you luck in your dispute with the town.

Evan

If I was you I would just stop teaching Darwin and teach what you are supposed to teach. I don't think you should continue this trial. If you stop, you could get away with it and nothing would happen to you. If you don't stop, you could lose your job and your girl will leave you.

Dominic

I am sorry you are in all this trouble. My advice to you in this situation is not to take it back, stand up for what you believe in. About the girl, if she loves you at all she will stick by you no matter what happens. If she doesn 't, then she probably doesn't love you as much as you think. The church is standing up for what it believes and so should you. If you back down now, what will the future bring? Anyone will fight against something they don 't like and there will be no freedom. You will have to decide what you should do. Nobody can make that decision for you. Weigh your options; you will realize that some things are more important than others. Even I can 't tell you what you should do. I can only give you suggestions. Only you can make that decision.

Jennifer

These letters generate lively discussion about the issue of free speech and about what students think Cates should do. Students then read the rest of the play with a greater sense of discovery and pleasure, delighted when they find their predictions fulfilled or angry when Cates takes a course of action with which they disagree. In either case they are personally involved in the play. Similar activities can enhance the study of many other works of fiction. For example, students can give advice to Gene Forrester in *A Separate Peace* on how to deal with his rivalry with Finny or with his guilt after the accident; they can advise Kino in *The Pearl* about what to do with the pearl after the pearl buyers deny him a fair price and his wife wants him to throw the pearl away. Students have to consider the facts of the stories in new ways and become active readers in order to respond intelligently. We build on our students ' proclivity for giving advice by offering them the opportunity to become "experts" on issues that are of interest to them. We tell them they will share their expertise with other students in the school as part of an Issues Fair.

To begin this activity, we conduct an interest survey to help our students identify the issues that concern them the most. They usually include such topics as nuclear power, environmental pollution, careers, motherhood, drugs, alcoholism, AIDS, capital punishment, abortion, and war. The class members are divided into groups based on their responses to this interest survey. Students indicate their first, second, and third choices. We try to place students in their first-choice group, but in order to have groups of no more than four students, and to assure a mix of student abilities and talents in each group to permit successful completion of the tasks involved in the final presentation, we may have to give a few of them their second or even third choice. We also want each group to include at least one student with leadership qualities and at least one with some artistic talent.

To begin the project, we ask students to describe in their journals what they already know or believe about the issue they will explore. Because these are issues they have chosen as important to them, they already have opinions and knowledge, sometimes even first-hand knowledge. Based on their journal entries, they discuss the issue in their groups, share their knowledge, and decide what else they need to know to become experts.

Recognizing the appeal of primary research for all students—but particularly for the disenchanted, who often have an antipathy for library research—we direct our students to local sources of information in the school and in the community. For example, students interested in environmental issues can begin right in school by talking with the advisor to the Environmental Awareness Club, who, in turn, will direct them to community resources. Students interested in exploring the implications of alcohol or drug abuse can begin by talking to the school's substance abuse counselor, contacting the local chapters of MADD (Mothers Against Drunk Driving), SADD (Students Against Drunk Driving), VAASE (Varsity Athletes Against Substance Abuse), and AA (Alcoholics Anonymous). Our town's police department, elected officials, clergy, and even local lawyers and physicians are usually willing to work with our student researchers. Of course their cooperation is predicated upon our students knowing how to make and keep appointments and conduct productive interviews.

The best way we have found to prepare students for these interviews is to model the process. We invite an expert on an issue that interests us to come to our class to be interviewed. For example, one time Marcia invited the chairperson of the local agency working to combat discrimination in our community. In preparation for this visit Marcia reviewed with the class what she already knew and what she needed to know. She wanted more information about the extent of the problem, ways our community is addressing it, the attitude of residents toward discrimination against religious, ethnic, racial, and other minorities, financial resources available to the guest's organization, and techniques the speaker has developed for overcoming discrimination. Marcia told the class that as she interviewed her guest, other questions might occur to her. She also explained that she would be taking notes for this interview, but that she could have chosen to use a taperecorder. However, she added, she would never tape-record a conversation without first asking permission of her guest.

The day of the interview, Marcia arranged a table and two chairs in the front of the classroom. She introduced the guest to the class and invited her to sit down. She then asked the guest most of the questions she had prepared. However, she also allowed the guest to pursue areas of interest to her, such as the need for sensitivity training for teachers and students to promote understanding among groups in the school and in the community.

At the end of the interview Marcia thanked her guest for her time and for her willingness to share her expertise. Modeling an interview takes most of a class period, but for many students, especially the disenchanted, seeing the entire process helps them learn how to conduct themselves when they go out into the community to do their research.

At this point our students are ready to begin their own research. To facilitate the process, they review in their groups what they need to know about their issues and the initial sources of information available to them. They divide the responsibility for collecting data among themselves. We allow class time for them to make appointments and to conduct the interviews. If they go off campus, special arrangements must be made with the school administration and parents. We provide the permission forms but put the responsibility for getting approval on the shoulders of the students.

After they have collected their information and recorded it in their journals, they meet to discuss their findings. They exchange journals and then comment in writing on the recorded information. In this way students get feedback on their work and discover what additional information is needed.

When their research is completed, usually within a week, each group must produce a pamphlet reporting on its issue. Because we have the technical capability, we encourage our students to use one of the available computer publishing programs to create a professional-looking product. Here's where the artistically talented student can successfully team up with a computer-literate group member. One group explored alcohol abuse and produced a pamphlet on fetal alcohol syndrome (FAS), which included this profile:

Glenda is short, her head is too small for the rest of her body, and her eyes are misshapen. The middle part of her upper lip is woefully thick, and her jaw juts forward. Her body is twisted by scoliosis and she wears a hearing aid because she is partially deaf. Glenda's mother was an alcoholic. Glenda suffers from the devastating effects caused by the alcohol her mother consumed before she was born. She is permanently disabled because of Fetal Alcohol Syndrome or FAS, which is becoming a major medical concern for all Americans.

Fetal Alcohol Syndrome does not concentrate in one economic level. It cuts across all economic boundaries. Mrs. Deborah Disanza, a Student Assistance Counselor for our school, believes that people are not willing to recognize the fact that FAS is more widespread than we think. She told me that according to the March of Dimes, one out of every 750 newborns, or about 5,000 babies per year, has FAS. FAS was officially identified in the United States in 1973 by doctors at the University of Washington. FAS is a combination of mental, physical, and behavioral defects that may develop in infants born to some women who drink heavily during pregnancy. FAS is among one of the three leading known causes of birth defects; also, it 's the leading cause of mental retardation. Some of these birth defects consist of prenatal and postnatal growth deficiency. A particular pattern of facial malformations, such as a small head circumference, flattened midface, sunken nasal bridge, and a flattened and elongated philtrum (the groove between the nose and upper lip). The central nervous system can be severely damaged, which can result in mental retardation. Alcohol withdrawal symptoms at birth can include a poor sucking response, sleep disturbances during early infancy, restlessness, short attention span, and hyperactivity. Malformations in the body 's major organs can also result from FAS. These include muscle problems, defects in the bones and joints, genital defects, and kidney abnormalities.

There is no treatment for an FAS child, reported Dr. David Ingall, professor of pediatrics at Northwestern Medical School. "The damage has been done before birth." FAS babies can never catch up mentally or physically with normal babies. Of 95 million Americans who drink, at least 2 million of these people are women of childbearing age. In 1975, a nation-wide survey of teenage drinking patterns revealed one third of all girls are moderate to "heavy" drinkers.

There may not be a treatment or safe dose to prevent FAS, there is certainly a way to prevent it. When a woman is planning a pregnancy she should stop drinking before attempting to conceive and should continue to abstain throughout the pregnancy and nursing. Women who drink and have an unplanned pregnancy should stop as soon as they suspect that they are pregnant. Before a woman may realize she is pregnant the baby's brain, heart, and other organs begin to form and are especially vulnerable to damage from alcohol.

Alcoholism is a chronic, progressive and potentially fatal disease characterized by tolerance and physical dependency. You can't expect an infant to cope with problems brought upon him by his alcoholic mother. Children have a right to live healthy and normal lives. They deserve a fighting chance at life, starting from conception. To have that chance, young women need to be made aware of the effects of alcohol on their unborn babies and STOP DRINKING!

A group concerned about the nation's rising crime rate argued for the reinstitution of the death penalty:

In 1972 the U.S. Supreme Court ruled that the death penalty was unconstitutional. The consensus ruling was that the death penalty itself was not unconstitutional but the way it was used is. The Court said the random and discriminatory way it was used made it unconstitutional. But they still reaffirmed our belief that the death penalty is right to use when used correctly. In 1976 the death penalty was reaffirmed by the Supreme Court Guidelines.

The major question about the death penalty is whether or not it is a deterrent to crime. There are two kinds of deterrents. One is to prevent people from committing any further crimes. The death penalty most definitely prevents a person from committing any further murders because a dead person cannot commit the same offense over and over again. Criminal Justice graduate Thomas DeLuca agrees, saying, "Criminals who prove they can not be rehabilitated by repeating criminal offenses must be put to death for the good of society."

The other kind of deterrent is the prevention of a crime before it happens. In America today the death penalty is not a very good deterrent to crime. There are many reasons for this. According to *Criminal Justice*, only 37 of the 50 states have the death penalty. In order for it to work, a united front is needed. Another reason is that there are just too many delays in our court system. There are many appeals on every case as well as the filing of habeas corpus petitions that cause the cases to take years to get through the courts. According to *Newsweek*, of the 2,400 convicts on death row only 121 have been executed. The delays have taken away the effectiveness of capital punishment as a deterrent. For capital punishment to be a real deterrent the murderer must know execution will be certain and swift upon conviction.

Ernest Preate, the Attorney General of Pennsylvania, said about our legal system that it is so complex that it "stands in the way of the imposition of the death penalty even when validly imposed. Unnecessary delays and countless reviews frustrate the will of the majority. These delays and reviews must be reduced if the death penalty is to be a viable deterrent." Chief Justice William Rehnquist, in an article in *The Nation*, calls these delays "a serious malfunction in our legal system."

A look at Canada 's experience after abolishing the death penalty reveals just how much of a deterrent to crime capital punishment really is. According to *Law Without Order*, in 1967 when Canada still had the death penalty, there were 129 murders per 100,000 people. Just one year after that there were 314. The crime rate rose dramatically in big cities too. In Quebec the crime rate rose by 17%. Murder went up by 47%. In Ontario, murder rose by 71%; rape went up by 20%, and assaults were up 14%.

We strongly believe that the death penalty is right and could be a deterrent to crime if it were used properly. The death penalty could be a great help in the war on drugs. If we started to execute drug dealers, there would not be as many people wanting to be dealers. There should also be death for all convicted murderers. Right now the average murderer only gets seven years in jail. If we executed all murderers the crime rate would decrease greatly. As for the long delays in court, there should be a limit on appeals so that executions can be carried out swiftly. We realize with executions there would be some mistakes, but in the long run the death penalty would lower the crime rate and save the lives of so many innocent victims. If the executions could be brought out from behind prison walls and into the public eye where potential criminals could see them, they might think twice before committing another crime. Effective use of the death penalty is in our opinion the only thing that can deter the murderer, kidnapper, rapist or drug dealer.

In recent years our students have become much more concerned about alcohol abuse among young people, so we have included here another sample pamphlet related to alcohol abuse, this time from a group addressing the issue of drunk driving:

Many studies by experts show that drunk driving is on the increase among teenagers. The National Council on Alcoholism said that drunk driving is the leading single cause of death among fifteen to twenty-four year olds. Twenty-five thousand of them die each year in drunk driving accidents. Five thousand of those victims are teenagers. The *Editorial Research Report* tells us that 40% to 60% of all fatal crashes involve teenaged drunk drivers. And the numbers keep increasing. For all traffic crashes, young drivers are more likely to have been drinking than older drivers.

A teenager is four times more likely to have an alcohol related accident than any other driver. 92% of high school students have used or tried alcohol. 14% of that drinking is done in cars. Drivers between the ages of 16 and 24 have twice as many fatal crashes per mile driven as older drivers. In December of 1990 a survey of students in our school was made on drunk driving. Fifty students were asked if drunk driving has increased. Of the fifty, twenty-five of them answered no. Thirty-three of the fifty said they feel it is all right to drive after drinking one beer, and only seven of the fifty students belong to SADD. That is why there is a problem with alcohol and driving in our town.

Because of the increase of drunk driving and its seriousness, legislation has been enacted in many states to combat the problem. The laws include raising the drinking age to twenty-one years, marking of licenses of drivers under twenty-one, and increasing the penalties for DWI offenders. Along with the laws there are organizations that try to prevent drunk driving.

- MADD (Mothers Against Drunk Driving) is composed mainly of victims of drunk drivers and their relatives. MADD, an organization with many groups across the nation with a lot of members, has persuaded Hallmark Cards to stop producing and shipping cards that link graduation and alcohol. MADD claims there are more people graduating under twenty than any other age group.

- SADD (Students Against Drunk Driving), has chapters at some 7,500 high schools, including ours. The group advisor, Ms. DiSanza, wishes more people would join. She said, "Kids feel if they join they won't be allowed to drink." Ms. DiSanza also said, "SADD is there to let people know about the problem, and there is no way to see it helping because there is always a roller coaster of how many people join."

- RID (Remove Intoxicated Drivers). This is the first national group dedicated to getting drunks off the road.

- BACCHUS (Boost Alcohol Consciousness Concerning the Health of University Students). It started in 1976 and has 183 chapters. This group also has campaigns to ban or restrict beer and wine commercials on television and radio. All these organizations are trying to reduce the number of teenagers killed and injured in alcohol related accidents.

Drunk Driving is increasing throughout the nation, but there are ways it can be stopped:

- Friends have to be aware of friends drinking.
- Take the keys of the car away from a drunk friend.
- If your friends drink, don 't let them drive.
- Call Safe Rides to get someone else to take you home.

Drunk driving is dangerous to your health. It can kill you. Don't wait for something bad to happen to make your friends know the seriousness of the problem. And remember: DON'T DRINK, but if you do, DON'T DRIVE!

To generate interest in the issues the students have researched, we have them create a poster approximately 30 x 25 inches that will become the focal point of their exhibit at the Issues Fair, to which we invite students from other classes. Each group creates a table display advertising its issue with a poster, slogans, and signs. They speak as experts when visiting students ask questions about that issue, and they hand out copies of their pamphlet, which we have duplicated for that purpose. Visiting students are always impressed with the work represented in the fair. For many of our disenchanted students this event is the first opportunity (in high school, at least) for them to be recognized as knowledgeable, successful students. For example, the group that focused on drunk driving produced a dramatic display sign (see page 41) that attracted many students to listen attentively to their classmates and read the pamphlet with obvious interest. The Issues Fair always reminds us of how well our students learn from each other when given the opportunity.

Grading the project can present us with some challenges. We give a group grade based on our assessment of the overall presentation. But we also give individual grades based on each student 's contribution to the group effort. To help us assess this contribution, each group submits a portfolio of work leading to the presentation and an indication of which students worked on which aspects of that presentation. Student journals also become part of this portfolio and assist us in the assessment process.

The Issues Fair takes approximately three to four weeks to complete, and we believe it is worth every bit of that time. A fair is also an appropriate forum for students to share information with each other about books they have read. This is especially true in a whole-language environment in which students are reading separate titles. We group students as we did for researching issues, to create learning-log partners. Students respond to their books as they read them, and their partners comment, question, and make suggestions in their logs. The goal here, in addition to getting students to think and write about the experience of reading their books, is to inform and interest their classmates in the books they have read. To do this, they assume the persona of the author who is interested in selling her or his book to a high school audience. As such, each "author" must tell something about the characters and the plot in order to interest potential readers but not give too much away.

Jeanine assumed the persona of Stephen King:

My book, *Carrie*, is one of the weirdest and best I have ever written. Knowing how much much you all enjoy my novels, I am sure you will absolutely love this book. It's scary, the main character is about your age, it 's not too long, it's very exciting and always a lot of action is going on. All this is in one novel, and it's very easy to understand.

Before you can even follow this book, you have to understand about Carrie's special power. She is telekinetic, which means she can move objects and start fires with her mind. All Carrie has to do is picture something happening in her mind, and it will happen.

The first really weird experience that happens is when Carrie blows out a light bulb with her power. The reason she does this is that the girls in her gym class were antagonizing and teasing her. They made her very upset and hurt. She started to cry, but that just made the girls laugh and tease

No Cruisin'

Yellow

Red

After Boozin'

her more. When Carrie's temper gets started, she can't control herself. Then all of a sudden the light bulb above her exploded and shattered all over the other girls. This was the first time the students at school witnessed her powers.

Another strange and horrifying time Carrie revealed her powers was at her senior prom. Most students thought she was very strange and didn 't deserve to go to the prom. One of the girls in her senior class decided to play a cruel and nasty joke on Carrie. The student dumped a bucket of pig 's blood all over Carrie in front of everyone at the prom, but the joke backfired against all the students because Carrie felt they should all be punished for the way they had treated her all her life. She made many things happen, like starting fires and causing explosions, which led to the deaths of most of the students at the prom. It was a terrible tragedy.

I know I 've told a great deal about the story, but that won't ruin the book for you because there are many more horrifying details. This book has it all. I think you would really enjoy reading it. I know I enjoyed writing it.

Kevin presented himself as Tom Clancy:

Today I am here to tell you about the book I have written, *Red Storm Rising*. My book tells a tale of war and the politics behind it. This book shows the cruelty of man and the lack of human feeling of the politicians who play with soldiers' lives.

The value of learning about the horrors of war may save lives and spare the families the grief and pain of mourning the dead. My book shows how it might be, from the front lines to the people trapped behind enemy lines, if the super powers of the world fight. At one point in the book, an Air Force lieutenant along with three marines escape from their burning base and flee to the hills of Iceland. While on the run they find and capture a Russian patrol. They cut the Russians ' throats and put them in their truck to make the deaths look like an accident. This episode is just a small part of what the fighting forces of this country will see if they ever go to war in modern times.

I show that if a nation wants peace, it must be in control of the politicians that run the country. Otherwise, a small number of men can have the power to do whatever they want, even send their people to die for no good reason. For example, the Russian Politburo, rather than asking for the help of the west during an oil shortage, decides to go to war to get the oil reserves and make it look like they were not the aggressors. To do this, they plant a bomb in the Kremlin and kill a group of young Vitroberists, the Russian version of the Boy Scouts. Then they have a German double agent take responsibility so they can use the incident as a reason for war, in which they even want to use nuclear weapons rather than lose.

In this book I show the value in knowing about the horrors of war and why they should be avoided at all cost. I also show the value of the people of a nation having more say in the actions of the governments. I wrote beyond just telling a story of war between two great and powerful nations; it is a warning to the world.

Sometimes, when given choices in their reading, students may even select and enjoy a "classic." Elizabeth read *Ethan Frome* and presented herself as Edith Wharton:

> Good afternoon students and Mrs. Lubell. Thank you for inviting me here to speak about my latest novel, *Ethan Frome.* I chose to write about Ethan because he is a man who is stuck in the life he is living. His wife, Zeena, is bitter and cranky, not to mention a hypochondriac, and she brings no joy to his life whatsoever. He also has the burden of a dying mill and unproductive farm. The one thing that brings Ethan happiness is his wife 's cousin, Mattie Silver, who is the total opposite of Zeena. Mattie is sweet, charming, and beautiful. Since Mattie has no place to go and doesn 't have any other family or skills, she lives with Ethan and Zeena. Ethan and Mattie go for walks together at night and she makes him forget about his worries. But when Zeena's latest doctor tells her she is terminally ill, Zeena forces Mattie to move out so she can house a hired nurse. Coincidence? Maybe. Now the story begins. Ethan and Mattie are forced to separate. For Ethan, this means he 'll have only his bitter wife to talk to and he will have nothing left in his life to enjoy. And Mattie has nothing else in her life besides Ethan. She cannot handle any job and doesn 't know anyone else so they will do *anything* to stay together, even if it means they are together in death. I will not tell you any more except that there is a very unexpected and ironic twist at the end that will completely throw you.
>
> In this story, I was trying to tell my readers that sometimes a person is bonded to his destiny and nothing, not even death, can break him free from it. Also, I wanted to show that what a person dreams of is what he might already have and what he is trying to escape from is what he is escaping to. Sounds peculiar, huh? Well, you'll just have to read my novel to figure it out!

Students become very involved with this activity, dressing up for the part, using appropriate props, even dramatizing scenes from their books. We limit initial presentations to five minutes and videotape them so we can replay them for the students and for ourselves as we evaluate each performance. Students also rate each presentation anonymously. Based on these ratings, we select five authors to appear as part of a Meet the Authors panel. For this presentation the "authors" prepare answers to questions from students submitted in advance. Questions may also be asked from the floor. As with the initial presentations, we videotape the panel discussion. We also encourage students to borrow the videotape to review on their own and to show their families. For some parents this video is the only exposure they have to what is happening in the classroom.

"Advice and Consensus" engages our students on many levels in activities they recognize as relevant to them. They appreciate the challenge of real work for real audiences and the opportunities for classroom interaction as well as community involvement. We like the unit because students engage in critical thinking as they draw on their natural curiosity and creativity to take responsibility for their own learning.

KID LIT

Anyway, I keep picturing all these little kids playing some game in this big field of rye and all. Thousands of little kids, and nobody's around—nobody big, I mean—except me. And I'm standing on the edge of some crazy cliff. What I have to do, I have to catch everybody if they start to go over the cliff. . . . That's all I'd do all day. I'd just be the catcher in the rye and all. I know it's crazy, but that's the only thing I'd really like to be.

Holden Caulfield, *from* Catcher in the Rye

J. D. Salinger

Teenagers and young children seem to have a natural affinity for each other—perhaps because the teenagers, still close to childhood, are at the same time on the brink of adulthood. From the young child's perspective, a teenager is already a grownup who still remembers what little kids think and feel. The teenager also remembers what little kids like to do and has the energy and strength to do it. From the teenager's perspective, young children are innocent, untarnished incarnations of themselves: vulnerable, rambunctious, and full of creative possibilities. In other words, both groups tend to look at each other idealistically, ignoring warts and pimples.

Holden Caulfield's romantic view of children as innocent victims waiting to be sacrificed on the corrupt altar of a materialistic, hypocritical adult society is shared by many of today's teenagers. This perception explains why J. D. Salinger's novel *Catcher in the Rye* remains one of the most popular books high school students read. In our years of teaching, we have yet to meet a teenager who doesn't identify with Holden's desire to save innocent children from the corruption of adult society. If that identification proves true for average teenagers, it is even more true for disengaged students, who may see themselves as having been betrayed by the adult world and are detached from the pedagogy of formal education. So we stimulate what is altruistic in these teenagers and challenge them to reach out to young children in ways that will enhance their primary school experience. We assure our high school students that in so doing they will have a positive impact on the lives of young children and, at the same time, learn some things about themselves.

At first the students, who either elect to take the course (which is preferable) or are assigned to it, generally protest their lack of knowledge of children or of children's literature. They all claim to suffer from amnesia about events and experiences of their early lives. We promise them their memory lapses are temporary and that we have the cure. To prove what we say is true, we begin the unit by asking students to introduce themselves and tell where they went to school in first grade. We sit in a semicircle. (If we had a carpeted floor, we would push the desks aside and sit on the floor, as young children do.) This arrangement adds to the informal atmosphere and lessens self–consciousness. Because everyone remembers the name of his or her first school, we achieve instant success with each student. We ask them to remember one—only one—detail about the school: the animals in the classroom, a characteristic of the teacher, a rule of behavior, the kind of cookies or juice served, a favorite playground game or piece of equipment, anything.

We begin this remembrance by sharing one detail from our first grade class: "My teacher, Miss Geraldine, had masses of curly red hair." We go around the room quickly, each student sharing, until it is our turn again, and we begin another round by sharing another remembered detail from first grade: "My best friend was a boy named Jimmy Joe." The students hadn't expected another round, but by now they're warmed up and beginning to remember a few details. The sharing stimulates more memories. We let this process continue until either it begins to wind down or 10 minutes remain in the period.

At this point we ask students to jot down on notebook paper all the details they remember from their first grade. They are not writing a composition to be handed in, and they needn't worry about syntax, language mechanics, or form; they are just to record what they remember.

Before the end of our first period together we tell students how wonderful their memories are—and they are—and that we're looking forward to hearing more from them. We also tell them to get a journal (an 8 x 10 spiral notebook works well for this purpose), one that will be used exclusively for this course and that they must bring to class every day—in fact, they should keep it handy all the time. However, we offer the classroom file cabinet as a safe journal repository for students who have a history of losing journals. This journal, we emphasize, *cannot* be lost; it is essential for the work we do in this course.

The first day in Kid Lit is critical for success, especially for disenchanted students. An atmosphere of acceptance and interest in the individual, important in any class, must be established immediately in this class. Disenchanted students expect "the same old thing" from an English course, which means to them an assignment to read a book selected by the teacher, answer questions about the book asked by the teacher, and then write a composition on a topic created by the teacher. None of these teacher-centered activities is likely to engage the disenchanted. For them, English is a game in which they have no personal investment, the outcome of which is predetermined to meet some arcane criteria known only to the teacher. And they view the teacher as someone who has all the right answers, which they must figure out in order to win the game. The obvious way for disenchanted students to rebel is to disengage from the game. Our task as teachers is to reengage these students by giving them an opportunity to help design a new kind of game, one in which they have a personal investment and from which they receive immediate rewards.

We lay the groundwork for that personal investment by enlisting the assistance of the principal and staff of a nearby primary school. We ask all the first grade teachers (there are five in our neighborhood school) to allow four or five high school students to become big brothers and sisters to the children in each class during the weeks of Kid Lit. When we initially proposed this high school–primary school cooperation, we met with the primary school principal to discuss our proposal and to enlist his support and that of his kindergarten, first-, and second-grade teachers.*

We described the course's, goals and objectives and asked for the principal's suggestions for making the course educationally and personally worthwhile for all the students and teachers.

We have included the general course description, the attendance record forms, and sample letters on pages 70–72. We might have written a more detailed course description, one that outlines daily lessons, but we resisted the temptation because if we had, our high school students would have had fewer opportunities to design the activities of the course around their interests and those of the primary school children with whom they work. We didn't worry about offering sufficient opportunities for students to practice the language skills of reading, writing, listening, and speaking inherent in any worthwhile, comprehensive English course. We knew we could weave these skills into the fabric of each day's activities. From the first day, we practiced a variety of language activities as students spoke, listened, wrote, and read about their first-grade memories.

On the second day we greet students at the classroom door. (We also tell them good-bye at the end of each period to indicate our respect for them. We are models for our students, just as they will be models for the primary school children with whom they will be working.) We tell them they will need their journals that day and every day from then on. However, we are prepared to hand out paper to those students who forgot to get a journal. We ask them to respond to the journal topic we have written on the chalkboard:

> Tell about one unforgettable experience you had in primary school. Try to remember what you saw, heard, touched, tasted, smelled, and especially how you felt. Be as specific as you can.

---

* We had previously received course approval, including the proposed high school–primary school liaison from our high school principal. We also made sure we had legal approval for the high school students to walk to the primary school or, with parental approval, drive to the school from the technical center. (Many of the disenchanted are technical students who seek out practical educational programs for which they receive more immediate and tangible rewards than they usually do from traditional programs.) If the elementary school were not within walking distance from the high school, we would have arranged for periodic busing of students to and from the primary school. This arrangement obviously requires more teacher involvement in scheduling, but teachers can enlist the cooperation of students to create a busing schedule.

Because of our round-robin discussion in the previous class period, this is not a difficult topic; the students are primed. We, too, are eager to write on this topic. In fact, we write in our journals every day right along with our students; we are both sharing the experience of remembering our childhood and modeling a process:

- We get to work immediately. We don't wait for the bell to ring to begin, nor do we expect students to leap up from their seats like Pavlov's dogs the instant the bell signals the period's end.
- We focus on the topic for 5 to 10 minutes, unhampered by attention to language mechanics.
- We use our journal writing to help us remember our childhoods and to think on paper.

We read our students' journal entries from time to time, responding to content only to identify those memories or discussions that have the potential to become good stories. We "grade" the journals, but only as they reflect diligence and some thought to the writing. Most journals earn an A or a B; those journals to which we assign a C are either perfunctorily written or missing some entries.

On the first few days of journal writing we assign the topics, but after that we usually invite the students to write about any other childhood memory they wish. At first only one or two students pick up on this option, but gradually others begin to generate their own topics, sometimes suggesting them for the class. We encourage this participation because some of our most valuable journal entries come from student-generated topics, such as the one proposed by Rachel:

■   Tell about a time you stole something.

Rachel got so involved with this topic in her journal that later in the course she decided to use it as the basis of a short story to share with the first-grade children with whom she was working.

Every day that the class meets, students find a journal topic on the chalkboard, one we have suggested or one a class member has proposed. Within a few days the pattern of writing is established: Students and teacher write in their journals for a few minutes at the beginning of the period. Then we ask students to share their journal entries. Often they're hesitant to do so, but when we remind them that they shared some memories during the previous class, usually someone will start to read. Sometimes we have to begin the sharing, and that will motivate other others to join in. We don't force it though; we encourage sharing and respond as positively to the content (never mentioning organization, form, or mechanics) as we would to a friend or a guest in our home who shared a childhood anecdote with us. Our purpose now is to establish an environment of acceptance and encouragement. The time to help students with form and language mechanics is later, when they are using their journal entries as the basis for stories or poems for their primary school audience. At that point they will be much more receptive to suggestions for revision and correction.

We don't spend much time sharing journal entries on the second day of class because we want to prepare the students for their introductions to the children and the cooperating teachers. We have arranged for the initial visits on the third or fourth day of class. Ideally, four or five high school students are assigned to one elementary class so that each high school student can work with four or five children (depending on the class size) on a regular basis and develop a close relationship with them.

Before creating student groups, we make our initial visit to the elementary school, where we meet the principal, take a brief tour of the building (including the cafeteria and the playground) and end up in the library. Here we have arranged for the students to meet the librarian, who tells them about the kinds of books young children generally like and about three or four of their favorite titles. This first visit to the library is very important because one of the requirements for the unit is that high school students must read and review at least six books appropriate for primary-age children. We keep the book review format simple:

BOOK REVIEW FORM FOR WRITING FOR CHILDREN

Use Narrative form. Give *title, author, publisher, and date of publication.*

Intended age level

Brief plot summary

Description of characters (people, animals, imaginary creatures, other)

Setting (realistic, historic, fantasy, combination, other)

Purpose (entertain, teach, provide a moral lesson)

Illustrations (e.g., drawings, photographs, pictures, etc.)

Evaluation

The purpose of the review is to encourage students to read some of the children's best-loved books so they will know what appeals to "their" youngsters. Obviously our students can benefit from this information when working with the children and, more important, when writing for them.

On the day after our initial visit to the elementary school we assign the following journal topic:

■ Tell how you felt about being back in elementary school.

The 10 minutes of writing time is always followed by an animated discussion of shared memories and reactions. If occasionally some students are reluctant to respond, we ask them to describe their sense of the size of the hall, the cafeteria, the chairs, the playground, the library, and themselves as compared to their memories. We also ask them to react to the books the librarian told us were popular with primary school students. That prompts a lively discussion of what is a good book for young children and what they remember as their favorite books. As always, we share *our* memories and reactions.

In the next class session we build on this involvement with children's books as the basis for a journal entry. We write on the board:

> Tell about your favorite childhood book or story. Be sure to include your reactions to the story and the storyteller, if the book was read to you.

We tell the students to take some extra time with this topic and that we will collect their journals at the end of the period—not to grade them, but only to read them to see how they're doing. Our personal journals will be available for students to read if they wish. Then we all write for about 15 minutes. We stop the writing when we sense that students have had their say. We collect the journals and promise to return them at the next class session. We always keep that promise because our students, especially the disenchanted, need immediate personal feedback from us. We are careful when responding to these journals to comment only on their content and as one person talking to another. For example, here's an entry from Kiri's journal:

> The only time I came anything close to stealing something was a time when I went food shoping with my mom it was on a Saturday I remember because every Sat was food shoping day. We, me and my mom, were in the fresh fruit and vegetable isle and my mother started to eat the grapes that were on display, naturaly I started to eat them thinking it was O.K. since my mom was eating them. But I was wrong because my mom took me to one of the managers and told them I had stolen and eaten thier grape. When I tried to defend myself by telling them my mom had ate them also, my mom cameback with the excuse that she was just testing them to see if they were OK to buy.
>
> (Teacher Response:) I bet that was the sourest grape you ever ate. How did you feel when your mother said she was just testing the grapes? What did you say to her afterward? This could be the basis of a story if you add dialogue between you and your mother.

Obviously we ignored all syntactical and mechanical errors. The purpose of the journal is not to promote mechanical accuracy but to stimulate thought and fluency of language. We have another goal in this first reading of journals: We want to ascertain the scope of our students' language fluency and depth of thought. Reading their first four journal entries—which include their reactions to the primary school visit and their remembrances of school and of favorite books—gives us insight not only into our students' facility with language but into them as people. We then assign teams based on this first view of them, on their interaction in the high school classroom, on any strong feelings they have expressed for or against a particular elementary school teacher, and on our observations of them. We try to mix the students on the basis of gender and their varying language and social abilities. Obviously, a student more capable with written language can help others in his or her group who have difficulty with the written expression of ideas and incidents. For example, here is a journal entry written by Roy:

> Today I went to Mrs. Mazzela's class to read to the kids. I usually end up reading to boys, I guess because they like older kids of the same sex. The boys don't really care what we read. They pick out the books based on the color of the cover. They don't seem to know the expression "You can't judge a book by its cover." We read stories about people living today. But for the boys, the pictures were the most important thing about the book. I guess pictures help them understand what is happening. I remember reading all the Dr. Seuss books. Of course, at first they were read to me, and I just looked at the pictures. But it didn't take long for me to know from looking at those great pictures what was written on the page. I think that was how I learned to read. I know it was those pictures that got me interested in books. Anyway, everything went really well today and I had a good time.

Notice Roy's ability to describe his reactions to the school visit and to relate those reactions to memories of his early experiences with books. Roy's fluency and his ability to convey his personal voice enhanced his writing and helped him review stories written by his group members.

Now compare Roy's response to that of Tara, who obviously has difficulty expressing herself in writing.

> The classroom brought back alot of memories since I wentto that school when I was younger. I saw alot of things in the classroom like what I remember. But the classroom looks different, everything was so small. It brought back alot of memories.

Lacking Roy's facility with writtten language, her responses seem shallow and superficial. But there is much more to Tara than she was able to put into writing. She has a special talent for generating story ideas. Roy's fluency made his writing more readable, but his story ideas were not always appropriate for his audience of first-graders. In peer review sessions Tara's candid responses to Roy's contrived story ideas were invaluable. In the primary school classroom Tara's ability to tell a believable story that engaged the first-graders made her especially valued by her group and by Roy, who initially had difficulty finding story ideas that appealed to his audience.

Grouping students to work with the primary school children can seem formidable, but when we remember that we are grouping according to abilities that are not always measured by left-brained, verbal skills, then we see that Roy and

Tara had individual talents that complemented each other and enriched their experiences in writing for children.

Once the groups are formed, we establish a pattern of classwork generated by and enhanced by the primary school visits. Each group of four or five high school students has the responsibility to work out a visitation schedule (days and times) with the cooperating primary school teacher. If each group has a different schedule, we ask the elementary teacher to keep an attendance record and make weekly reports to us. Most teachers ask the students to sign in and out. The details of attendance are for each teacher to determine, in part depending on the policies of the school. What *is* important for this project to be successful is for high school students to have some involvement in working out the details of who visits whom and when. We put as much responsibility on them as we can. While accountability is measured in their attendance record, more validly it is placed on their reports, both oral and written, of what happens at each visit. Our students write a journal response after each primary school visit. Their early entries are sometimes tentative and lacking detail, as is Rachel's first entry:

> The kids wrote poems. We helped them with their spelling and helped them with their ideas. I was with three boys. One wrote about Teenage Mutant Ninja Turtles, one wrote about a train, and the other wrote about leopards. They had a lot of trouble spelling some words and lot of backward letters.

By her third visit Rachel has become more confident and anecdotal in her journal response:

> Today everybody in my group was paired up with a different first grader. We then went to the library, read a few poems to our partner and attempted to write a poem together. It didn't work out too well for me because my partner, Joey, kept changing his mind about what to write. It also took a long time for him to write anything because he wanted me to spell every word for him, even though I told him he didn't have to worry about spelling until later. Also, he has a very short attention span and I had trouble keeping him interested in writing the poem. I think he was more comfortable talking with me rather than writing. He also wanted to draw rather than write. As a result, we only wrote about three lines before we had to stop.

In addition to the primary school visits, things are happening in the high school classroom, including discussions about topics related to the students and their own childhood experiences. One of our early discussions takes place after our students' first primary school visit. We prepare for the day's discussion by offering the following as the journal topic:

> Tell about your favorite book as a young child. Tell why this book has special memories for you.

Occasionally, we have a few students who cannot remember a book from their early years, not even from school, so we encourage them to remember a well-loved film or TV program instead. We *try* to stimulate their memories of a book—either one they have read or one read to them—unfortunately books have had no place in some students' lives. As English teachers, we want to begin to change that, but we know we cannot accomplish that change by making our students feel inferior or inadequate. So we try to compensate by encouraging them to remember a TV program or film they particularly enjoyed.

We all write for about 10 minutes and then share our memories. As students begin to remember book titles and relive happy associations, more titles are identified. We begin to list the most popular ones on the chalkboard, noting what makes each book memorable. In a short time the list covers the entire board. When that happens—and before the enthusiasm of the discussion has begun to ebb—we ask students to review the list and try to categorize these best-loved or best-remembered books and the reasons for remembering them fondly. Throughout the unit we regularly stimulate our students to collect details about themselves as children and about the children with whom they are working—their interests, fears, dreams, questions, anxieties, and so on. We have them group the details, classify them, sequence them, and make generalizations about them. In so doing, we are enabling them to recognize relationships and discover purposes, the very heart of dialectics.

We remind the students of our purpose, writing for children, and tell them that as we collect details—apparently unrelated bits and pieces of events, dialogue, personal relationships, snatches of dreams, and remembered experiences—we are harvesting the raw material for the literature we are creating. The richer the details of our memories and experiences, no matter how apparently chaotic or trivial, the more successful will be our efforts to write for children.

By the middle of the second week of the unit, schedules for primary school visits have been established and the small groups have made plans to spend at least one class period with the children. In preparation for this visit we ask our students to note in their journals some of the questions they recall having had as children. These questions can be about anything: the natural world, relationships, sex, religion, history, and so forth. On the chalkboard we write:

> List the questions you used to have as a child—things you wondered about, wanted to know more about, or wanted to have explained to you, for example, "Where does the water in the bathtub go? Why do birds fly? How do fish breathe under water? Why did grandfather have to die? Are there animals in heaven?" and so on.

To prompt their reminiscences, we model the process by sharing some of the questions we had as children—for example, "What happens to the sun at night?" We also tell about the concerns we had that one day the sun wouldn't come back and the world would be dark forever. That scary thought generated lots of anxiety. We share all this with our students and then ask them to remember and write.

At the end of the writing time we ask them to review what they have listed and select the childhood question that was the most perplexing or troublesome to them. We do the same and write it on the board. We tell them we are going to remember where we were and what we saw, then draw a diagram or map of the setting and the circumstances surrounding the question. As we draw our memory map, other details come to mind and we add them. We remember whom we were with, to whom we asked the question, and how the person responded— or that we didn't ask the question and why not. We map the result of getting an answer or not and remember our feelings.

Ruth remembers lying in bed wondering what would happen if she put a hairpin in the electrical socket on the wall near her pillow. She sketches a crude line drawing of the bed with a child in it and of the electrical socket. The class thinks this is pretty stupid but funny.

They want to know what happened. She draws the socket and the fingers of the child holding the hairpin, about to insert it into the socket:

"Did you actually put it in?" they squeal.

She nods and then draws the face of sobbing child holding up two burned fingers:

"There was a loud pop, and all the lights in our apartment went out," she tells the students. "Then my mother rushed into my room to see if I was all right, I guess. After she had wiped my tears away and comforted me a bit, I told her I had burned my fingers." She draws the mother holding the child:

Ruth continues with the story: "She must have asked me how I burned my fingers, and I guess I told her. Anyway, she became very angry with me and yelled at me never to do such a stupid thing again." She draws the mother yelling:

Ruth then asks the class if they can guess why her mother got so angry. Their answers vary, but the story offers an opportunity to talk briefly about anger as a secondary emotion and what causes parents to get angry with their children, especially when they have endangered themselves in some way. Several students want to share similar stories. Ruth allows some sharing, but soon she returns to her story map, and tells the class what happened next. She shows the mother at the child's bed again, this time holding some ointment to relieve the pain of the burned fingers.

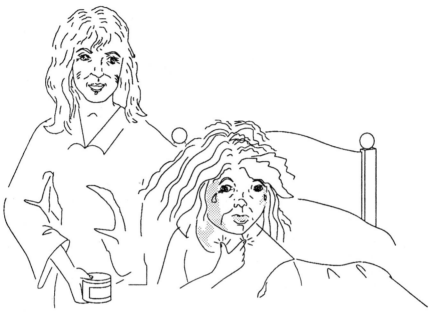

The mother tells her child that she is sorry she yelled at her, but that she was very frightened because what the child had done was dangerousand might have killed her. Ruth draws the frightened face of the child:

A student asks if the mother was right in telling the child she could have killed herself by sticking a hairpin in the electrical socket. The class discusses fear and its protective role in the lives of young children. Ruth says she understands that in this instance the mother deliberately frightened the child to protect her, and the tactic certainly worked, because she never again stuck anything other than a plug into a wall socket.

Finally Ruth draws the mother holding the child close to her, telling her that she loves her and that she is going to move the bed to a wall without an electrical socket on it.

This modeling and discussion have taken most of the period, but with the time left, students begin creating memory maps of their Question Story.

Another way of mapping is with words only. Ruth could have put the subject to be brainstormed in the center of the board and then drawn lines to other ideas and memories as they occurred to her, allowing these lines to branch off as other fragments of memory were generated. We often use this mapping technique to brainstorm ideas and stimulate memories. Students accustomed to linear, left-brain thinking may be initially uncomfortable with mapping and the apparent chaos of unexpected leaps and turns into memories.. However, for students who don't think in the conventional linear way—many of whom are among the disenchanted—mapping, especially a map that includes stick figures—is a liberating technique for reclaiming information stored in their memories.

Students use the memory maps to draft their personal stories, based on their own childhood questions, so we encourage them to write first-person narratives. But we also assure the students that their stories need not adhere strictly to the facts, that they are free to fictionalize their experiences for the sake of a better story, as long as the story rings true. This instruction leads to a discussion of the subtle difference between fact and truth in story telling. Our purpose here is not philosophical but practical. We want students to free their imaginations to tell good stories, ones that will not only entertain their young readers but also answer the questions that precipitated the events in the stories.

Once our students have completed the first drafts of their stories, they review them in their peer groups, reading aloud to each other and reacting to the stories. We move from group to group, listening, complimenting, asking a few questions, and occasionally making a suggestion. When the peer review is complete, we collect the drafts—not to grade, but to assess our students' narrative strengths and weaknesses. On each draft we comment on its content and make no more than two or three suggestions, most of which have to do with organization and language.

Most inexperienced writers don't know where to begin their stories and give too much background information before telling the real story. We suggest alternative beginnings and deletions of information that does not contribute to the story line. We also tell them that dialogue makes characters seem more true-to-life, and we encourage them to add some dialogue to their stories, assuring them that a writer has creative license to invent dialogue as long as it sounds believable for the characters speaking. Then we suggest some alternative words and phrases to replace the baby talk students sometimes affect when writing for young children. We do this sparingly and offer the changes only as suggestions; we will deal with the issues of appropriate language for children in our next class session, after we have returned the story drafts.

We begin our discussion of language for children's stories by reading brief excerpts from some of the titles our students have identified as their favorite books. We never know exactly what these will be, but we can predict that Maurice Sendak's *Where The Wild Things Are*, Dr. Seuss's *Cat in the Hat*, Roald Dahl's *The Wonderful World of Henry Sugar*, and E. B. White's *Charlotte's Web*, will be among them. Any titles by these authors (and many others—see page 67 for a recommended bibliography of children's books) will serve our purpose, but we like to refer to *A Wrinkle in Time* because its author, Madeleine L'Engle, has written and spoken extensively about the process of writing for children, and so we quote her. Like most of us, our students want to hear from the experts.

Ms. L'Engle says to writers that "writing is writing, whether the story is for the chronologically young or old. . . . Do not write it [your story] for children. Write it for yourselves. Write it for each other." We discuss the implications of this advice for our choice of topics and presentation of ideas, noting that L'Engle says "there is no idea that is too difficult for children as long as it underlies a good story and quality writing."

We also consider the implications of L'Engle's statements about language when we write for children. We listen to L'Engle's language in *A Wrinkle in Time* and to E. B. White's in *Charlotte's Web*. Then we listen to some simplistic, child-like writing. Unfortunately it's easy to find. Most supermarkets have copies of ill-conceived, poorly written children's books. We *never* read anything written by our students for this purpose; in fact, we never read anything by them we cannot compliment, nor do we read their work without permission. Comparing L'Engle's and White's rich language to the impoverished prose of the stories from the supermarket, we begin to understand that good writing *is* good writing regardless of audience and that to write down to children is writing down to ourselves, writing below our abilities.

We emphasize L'Engle's point that characterization, style, and theme are just as important in a story written for children as in one written for adults. The difference is that a child wants to read about another child, even one in animal form, having true-to-life adventures and dealing with realistic problems in a believable context. We hasten to add the obvious fact that this does not exclude fantasy, as long as it is believable in its presentation. Thus we are back to our initial topic of recognizing the difference between what is fact and what is truth, what is literal and what is believable. L'Engle's advice about believability and good writing becomes our criterion for success with this assignment. Now we send the students back to their drafts to begin revising—what we call the "real writing."

More peer reviews will follow, including an opportunity for students to "try out" their stories on the first-graders for whom they are writing. We will all agree on a final draft deadline, at which time stories will be submitted for evaluation. In addition to assessing our student's success with this assignment, we must also grade the stories. The students understand the criteria for grading, but we offer them the opportunity to revise their stories once more if they are dissatisfied with their grade. Together we determine a deadline for submitting revisions.

While we have been working on these first stories, the students have been visiting the primary school, reviewing children's books, and writing daily in their journals. The topics vary and are often suggested by class members, but we offer one to which students readily respond that can be the basis of the next story assignment: Tell about a fear you had as a child.

We write for 10 minutes and then share our fears. Ruth tells about her childhood fear of seeing the body of her grandmother in a casket. She remembers the feeling of her father's arms holding her up to look at the body, the sound of her mother's muffled sobbing, the oppressively sweet smell of flowers surrounding the casket, the salty taste of her tears, and her sense of shame because she knows she is crying for herself—out of fear and a compulsion to run out into the woods to hide from death.

On the board Ruth lists the sensory memories of sight, touch, sound, smell, and taste. Describing these sensory memories helps us to visualize the scene and understand, even identify with, her fear in looking at the reality of death. We want to know more about the incident: What was so frightening to her about the funeral? How long did she stay outside? Did her father come after her? How did her parents deal with her fears? Does she believe her parents could have dealt with those fears in a better way?

Ruth promises to provide the answers, but in the meantime she has the students review their journal entries and add as many sensory details as they possibly can. To help stimulate their memories, she tells the students to close their eyes and visualize the scene of their fear. She allows them time to overcome some self-conscious giggles and transport themselves into another time and place, into their childhood fear. She asks them to remember everything they see; after some seconds, everything they hear; after more time, everything they smell, everything they taste, and everything they can touch. Finally she asks them to remember what happened, how they felt, and what they did. She gives them time to remember and relive the experience.

Then she tells them to go back to their journals and write down everything they've just experienced, concentrating on sensory details. When they have finished, she tells them they have the material for a story about a childhood fear.

Before they begin drafting this story, we discuss point of view. Our first story, and certainly all our journals, are written in the first person; we are telling our own stories in our own personae. But now we may wish to create another character to take our place, one for whom we can more easily invent conflicts, outcomes, and dialogue. Some of our students are worried about this task. They are inexperienced and insecure writers; shifting the point of view and inventing story details seem beyond them. So we must model the process to relieve their anxieties and prompt their writing.

When it is feasible, we invite a professional writer of children's books to model her or his writing strategies. For example, Penelope Jones shared with one of Ruth's classes the development of her book *Holding Together*, a story about a child facing the death of her mother from cancer. Ms. Jones tells our students that the main character is really herself, that, in fact, writers re-create themselves in their heroines and heroes and that many of the details of school and home in the story came directly from her own experiences.

Ms. Jones also tells the students that her mother did indeed die from cancer, not when Ms. Jones was a child, but many years later, when she was grown. However, the pain of living with her beloved mother's illness and eventual death transcended time and age; so she was able to transfer that experience and her feelings to the little girl in the story. The father in the story was patterned after Ms. Jones's husband, whose relationship with his daughters became part of the book. Of course she had to invent the ending of the book to show how the fictional father dealt with his wife's death and his daughter's loss of a mother. Penelope says that wasn't difficult for her to do because she knew her characters so well that she could easily imagine their logical reactions.

Some of Ruth's students were intrigued with Penelope Jones's realistic descriptions of incidents in the classroom, on the playground, at a party, wherever several people are involved. They were curious to know how she could remember all the dialogue from her childhood. Ms. Jones confessed she couldn't remember the exact words; what she remembered were the incidents, and they prompted her to invent believable dialogue. She also told them she often had to invent incidents to serve the purposes of her story. Then she read a selection from the book and asked the students if they could tell what seemed "real" and what was invented. Of course they couldn't, because everything in the story seemed logical and believable. Penelope Jones's visit—like those of other professional writers who have from time to time visited the class—stimulated our students to work even harder on their stories, especially in creating dialogue and incorporating their own experiences into a fictional piece.

As we have been working on the story about a childhood fear, we are still writing daily in our journals, focusing on childhood incidents in which we experienced strong emotions. These journal assignments follow a pattern:

■ Tell about a time you felt lonely (or guilty, proud, embarrassed, especially cherished, happy, jealous, amused, heroic, content). Try to remember what you saw, heard, smelled, tasted, and touched.

To stimulate these memories, we may tell stories from own lives, read from children's books, or show short films (see bibliography on page 69). For example, *The Empty Tree House* is a film that deals with the loneliness of a young boy when his best friend moves away. *The Red Balloon*, a charming film about a special friendship between a little boy and a balloon, touches on several emotions. *Alone in the House*, as the title suggests, deals with a child's fear of being home alone after dark. Not only do these films stimulate student memories of experiences that generated strong emotional responses, but they show children reacting in various kinds of situations, thus providing rich material that students can use in their writings.

After our students have completed a number of journal entries detailing highly charged emotional situations, we show them how these memories can be transformed into short poems that primary school children not only will enjoy reading but can illustrate and even imitate. As before, we model the process, this time by reviewing the sensory impressions prompted by the film *The Empty Tree House*. We list several details of sight, sound, smell, taste, and touch. Then, as a class, we select those we think express the loneliness of the young boy in the film. The following is a sample poem:

Loneliness is gray
It smells like an abandoned tree house
It sounds like a silver whistle
It tastes like bitter tears
Loneliness feels like wet snow on cold cheeks

The class is always pleased with the group effort. We point out that in the first line the sight impression is transformed into a color, one that reflects the overall emotion, or mood, of the story. We also note the simple form of obvious similes for each additional line. We discuss the compression that the poetic form imposes on the film story, necessitating our careful selection of words to create strong images. Obviously the poem won't tell the whole story, but it will create a mood and suggest a context. It's then up to the readers to create their own stories for these images, which is why these "emotion poems" are effective story prompts for our high school students to share with their primary school children.

Using the group poem as a model, our students begin creating several emotion poems based on their journal entries. We encourage small-group cooperation, and we help our students select words and details to create images. The process goes well, and first drafts of poems are ready for peer review after a day or two. Revisions are made and final copies are printed and given to the primary school students who will illustrate them. The following represent several completed pieces:

Happiness is yellow
It sounds like children playing
It smells like wildflowers
It tastes like barbeque cooking
Happiness feels like the warm sun on a spring day

Anger is black
It sounds like screeching tires on a
*   hot tar pavement*
It smells like burning rubber
It tastes like dry sweat
Anger feels like grinding gears

Loneliness is gray
It sounds like the dull hum of a radio
It smells like a field of dead flowers
It tastes like salty tears
Loneliness feels like a stab in the back

Contentment is yellow
It sounds like the warm wind
It tastes like a ripe banana
It smells like sweet flowers
Contentment feels like a soft summer day

The culminating project in the course is a book written by each student for primary school children. The topic can be anything appropriate for the children with whom the students have been working. The book may be written for the children to read or to be read to them, or a combination of both, but it must be illustrated. This requirement is daunting to some students, but we alleviate their apprehension by assuring them they may (1) have an artistic friend do the illustrations, (2) use photographs, (3) engage a child artist, or (4) do simple drawings themselves, augmented with cutouts. Of course we show them samples of each method. However, we impress upon them the need to write a good story, one that is believable and appropriate for their audience.

We send the students to their journals to find story ideas.. Elex looked back at her journal entry telling about the time she was afraid. We suggested that she use that incident as the basis for her story. Because she wished to make some "plot" changes and add a character for the sake of dialogue, she decided to write her story in the third person. She considered presenting her main character as an animal, but she eventually decided to present him as a little boy, based on her primary school students' recommendation. When they reviewed the draft of the story, they didn't like the "people" being raccoons, especially because raccoons are masked bandits, they said. Besides, Elex was having difficulty with the illustrations, which she wanted to execute herself. She was unable to endow each raccoon in the story with individual characteristics, so she finally presented her characters as real people. Her story reflects the kind of final story students can be guided to create.

Shadows and Tall Trees

Kevin Brown sat on the floor of his bedroom, hoping that his parents would stay home that night, because he was afraid that the shadows would take him away. He couldn't tell his parents why he wanted them to stay home, because he knew that they wouldn't understand. So he got up and walked down the hallway to his parents' bedroom, hoping that he could talk them into staying home.

He opened the door and walked into the room. His mother was sitting on the bed polishing her nails.

"Hi mommy!" Kevin said.

"Hi sweetie, what are you doing?" asked his mother.

"Oh, I was just playing with my Tonka toys; where's daddy?"

"He's in the shower," answered his mom.

"So I guess you're still going out to dinner," Kevin said, obviously disappointed.

"Of course we are honey; we've been planning this for weeks now; you know that."

"I know but . . ."

"What's the matter, I thought you liked Susan," said Mrs. Brown.

"Oh no, it's not that. Susan is a great babysitter. It's just that when you and daddy go out at night, the, you know. . . shadows, the monsters come out," Kevin said, feeling ashamed that he let such things as shadows bother him. "Daddy won't be there to say the words to keep them away," added Kevin.

"Oh, is that all? Well, how about we have your father write them down so Susan can read them for you before she puts you to bed," suggested his mom.

"Could we really do that? Do you think it would work?"

"Of course it will," she said reassuringly. "Now go and play so I can finish getting ready; I'll talk to your dad when he gets out of the shower."

Kevin skipped out of the room and down the hall feeling better already. He went to his room and lined up his tonka toys and started to play again. He quietly rolled the trucks back and forth across his floor, listening to the quiet murmur that they made.

After a while, Kevin's dad came into his room with a pencil and piece of paper.

"Okay sport, let's get this show on the road," said Mr. Brown. He sat down on the bed and started writing on the paper.

SHADOWS BEWARE!
FOR YOU WILL NOT BOTHER
KEVIN TONIGHT

WE ARE WATCHING OVER
HIM AND YOU WILL NOT
GIVE HIM A FRIGHT, NOT
EVEN IF YOU BITE!
SO BEWARE AND BEGONE TONIGHT!!

Kevin watched intently as his father carefully printed the shadow monster words.

"Don't forget to tell Susan to read them to me before I go to bed," Kevin said anxiously.

"No, I won't forget; now go wash up for dinner."

Susan arrived a little while later and agreed to read the monster words to Kevin.

"Sure Mr. Brown, I won't forget to read them to him" Susan said.

"Okay, we'll be home around one o'clock," said Mr. Brown.

"Kevin has eaten already; all that has to be done is for him to take a bath before he goes to bed," Mrs. Brown instructed her.

"I know, I know and he has to be in bed by eight o'clock," Susan reassured Mrs. Brown. "Don't worry about us. We'll have a great time tonight, so have fun.

By eight o'clock Kevin was ready for bed and Susan was reading him a bedtime story.

"Okay Kevin, I said I'd read you one story. Now it's time to go to bed. It's after eight o'clock already," said Susan.

"Oh Susan, just one more story," pleaded Kevin.

"No, it's lights out time for you."

Susan got up and walked toward the door and turned off the light.

"Wait, you forgot to read the monster words," Kevin reminded her.

"All right, but after this you have to go to bed," Susan said as she turned the lights back on. "Where are they?" she asked impatiently.

"On my desk," answered Kevin.

Susan walked to the desk and picked up the piece of paper.
She glanced at the paper and started to laugh.

"Oh Kevin, you really don't believe in monsters, do you?" she asked still laughing.

"Well, of course, don't you?" Kevin asked bewildered.

"No, and even if there were, monster words wouldn't stop them," she said as she started to chuckle again.

Susan read the monster words in a dry, dull voice.
While she was reading, Kevin thought about what she had said.
Susan finished reading and turned out the light.

"Sleep tight and don't let the bed bugs bite," Susan said.

After Susan closed the door, there was only a trickle of light coming through the crack at the bottom of the door. Kevin got up to turn on his night light; when he did, there was a shrieking howl outside of his window. "It's just the wind," Kevin said to himself. He tried to turn on the night light, but it didn't work. With a sigh he climbed back in his bed and pulled the covers above his head. He lay awake for hours thinking to himself.

"What if the monster words don't work?" Kevin wondered. "That means that there is a monster out there waiting for me, waiting to eat me up. Well, there's only one way to find out!"

Kevin threw off the covers. He looked around amazed. His room was transformed into a world of shadows. Where the walls used to be, there was vast space. It seemed as though it would never end. There was a light in the distance and Kevin got up and walked towards it. It seemed to take him a long time to reach the light. When he got close enough to see it, he hid behind a weird sort of tree. He saw a giant fire with shadows dancing around the fire. He tried to move closer to the fire to get a better look, but he didn't want to be discovered. The shadows were talking in a language he couldn't understand. But then after a few minutes of listening to them, he began to understand what they were saying. He decided to be brave and walk out into the opening. When he did, the shadows stopped talking and stared at him. Up close they seemed to have no form at all. It was almost as if they were transparent. One shadow approached him and reached out to touch him. When the shadow touched him, all he felt was a cool breeze blow by him.

"Are you real?" asked the shadow.

"Of course I'm real!" Kevin answered. "Where am I?"

"Why, you're in your room; don't you recognize it?"

"If this is my room, what are you doing here?"

"We live here, just like you do," answered the shadow.

"Yes, we live here, but I don't understand what you're doing here; you're on the wrong side," replied another shadow.

"The wrong side? How can that be?" asked Kevin.

"Somehow you and your shadow got switched."

"Switched? Do you mean he's on the other side in my room?"

"Yes, yes my boy. Now stop asking so many questions," said the first shadow. We have to figure out how to get you back to the other side."

"I don't understand. You want to help me?" asked Kevin bewildered by the shadow's concern.

"Of course we do, why wouldn't we?" replied one of the shadows.

"Well, on the other side, shadows always frightened me. Why do you want to help me now when you tried to scare me before?"

"We never tried to scare you. The fear is in your mind. You're standing here with us now. Are you frightened?"

"No, I guess you're right. There was never anything for me to be afraid of," Kevin said.

"Now that's taken care of, let's try to get you home."

The shadows gathered in a big group and discussed ways to return Kevin to his home. They talked and talked for what seemed to be hours. And they finally came up with a solution. They walked back to Kevin's bed and told him the plan.

"Kevin, you have to do the exact same thing you were doing before you were transported here."

"Well, that's easy. I was in my bed with the covers pulled over my head."

"Then that is what you must do now."

Kevin climbed into the bed and yanked the covers over his head. "Okay, I'm ready." The shadows gathered around the bed and started to chant. "Wait," said Kevin. "Is this going to hurt?"

"Of course not. Now let us continue if you want to go home."

The shadows began to chant again and Kevin listened to their lulling voices until he began to fall asleep and their voices began to fade. When Kevin woke up later that night he was back in his room. He glanced at the clock thinking that he must have slept for an eternity. But it was only 12 o'clock. "What a weird dream," he thought to himself as he watched the shadows dance across his wall. Then he fell back to sleep.

After that night, Kevin never again had problems falling asleep. In fact, he liked to watch the shadows before he fell asleep and wonder if his adventure with them were a dream or if it had really happened.

Elex's story was written, edited, and corrected with care because it was based on a fear she had actually had as a small child. It was something she wanted to tell, and it was written for a real audience of young children whom the writer knew and respected. Elex needed no prompting to concentrate on her book because she was personally engaged in its production, just as she and all our students are personally involved in the content and planning of the course. In short, our students have been challenged to accept responsibility for their own learning, and they have risen to that challenge in remarkable ways.

Recommended Books for Young Children

Allard, Harry. *The Stupids Step Out.* Boston: Houghton Mifflin, 1977.

Andersen, Hans Christian. *Hans Andersen: His Classic Fairy Tales.* Transl. by Erik Haugaard. New York: Doubleday, 1978.

Bemelmans, Ludwig. *Madeline.* New York: Viking, 1977. (*We recommend all of the Madeline series.*)

Blume, Judy. *Freckle Juice.* New York: Dell, 1971.

Carle, Eric. *The Very Hungry Caterpillar.* New York: Puffin, 1984.

Carrick, Carol. *Some Friend!* New York: Clarion Books, 1979.

—————. *Stay Away from Simon!* New York: Clarion Books, 1985.

Cleary, Beverly. *Romona the Pest.* New York: Dell, 1982.

Clifford, Eth. *Help! I'm a Prisoner in the Library.* New York: Dell, 1981.

Collodi, Carlo. *The Adventures of Pinocchio.* New York: Scholastic, 1978.

Dahl, Roald. *The Wonderful Story of Henry Sugar and Six More.* New York: Bantam, 1979.

Fritz, Jean. *Where Was Patrick Henry on the 29th of May?* New York: Coward, Mc-Cann and Geoghegan, 1975.

——————. *Why Don't You Get a Horse, Sam Adams?* New York: Coward, Mc-Cann and Geoghegan, 1974.

Gag, Wanda. *Millions of Cats.* New York: Coward, McCann, 1977.

Gardiner, John R. *Stone Fox.* New York: Harper, 1983.

Harranth, Wolf. *My Old Grandad.* New York: Oxford Univ. Pr., 1984.

Hughes, Shirley. *An Evening at Alfie's.* New York: Lothrop, Lee & Shepard, 1985.

Hunter, Edith Fisher. *Child of the Silent Night: The Story of Laura Bridgman.* New York: Dell, 1984.

Jukes, Mavis. *Blackberries in the Dark.* New York: Knopf, 1985.

——————. *No One Is Going to Nashville.* New York: Knopf, 1983.

King-Smith, Dick. *Babe the Gallant Pig.* New York: Dell, 1983.

Lobel, Arnold. *Fables* New York: Harper, 1980.

——————. *Frog and Toad Are Friends.* New York: Harper, 1979.

MacLachlan, Patricia. *Sarah, Plain and Tall.* New York: Harper, 1985.

McPhail, David. *Henry Bear's Park.* Boston: Little, Brown, 1976.

Miles, Miska. *Annie and the Old One.* Boston: Little, Brown, 1971.

Moore, Lilian. *See My Lovely Poison Ivy.* New York: Atheneum, 1975.

O'Neil, Mary. *Hailstones and Halibut Bones.* New York: Doubleday, 1973.

Parish, Peggy. *Amelia Bedelia.* New York: Scholastic, 1970.

Paterson, Katherine. *Bridge to Terabithia.* New York: Avon, 1979.

Peterson, John. *The Littles*. New York: Scholastic, 1970.

Rey, H. A. *Curious George*. Boston: Houghton Mifflin, 1973.

Say, Allen. *The Bicycle Man*. Boston: Parnassus Press, 1982.

Sendak, Maurice. *Where the Wild Things Are*. New York: Harper, 1984.

Seuss, Dr. *If I Ran the Zoo*. New York: Random, 1980. (*Any Book by Dr. Seuss is excellent.*)

Silverstein, Shel. *The Giving Tree*. New York: Harper, 1964.

Steig, William. *Sylvester and the Magic Pebble*. New York: Simon & Schuster, 1969.

Thayer, Ernest. *Casey at the Bat*. Englewood Cliffs, NJ: Prentice Hall, 1964.

Thiele, Colin. *Storm Boy*. New York: Harper, 1978.

Viorst, Judith. *Alexander and the Terrible, Horrible, No Good, Very Bad Day*. New York: Atheneum, 1976.

White, E. B. *Charlotte's Web*. New York: Harper, 1952.

Williams, Margery. *The Velveteen Rabbit*. New York: Knopf, 1985.

Yashima, Taro. *Crow Boy*. New York: Puffin, 1976.

We also present films created for children to generate discussion with our students about the concerns of children and to examine ways that filmmakers have dealt with these topics. The following is a selected list of short films for young children:

After Dark. Media Group. *Deals with a child's fear of the dark.*

Bridge to Terabithia. Wilson. *Prompts discussion about death.*

The Fight. Disney. *Provides insight into fighting.*

Loneliness: The Empty Tree House. Xerox. *A film about loneliness.*

The Lorax. BFA Educational Media. *Animated presentation of the consequences of environmental irresponsibility.*

Lost Puppy. Churchill Films. *Examines the reasons for rules.*

Lunch Money. Disney. *Deals with stealing.*

The Red Balloon. CCM Films. *Tells the story of a boy's special friendship.*

Stone Soup. Weston Wood Studios. *A fantasy with a lesson.*

Course Description

"Kit Lit" is a course/unit in which high school students create stories, poems, even short plays for young children. In order to know their audience, their interests, their feelings, fears, fantasies, etc., the high school students will read children's literature and visit the elementary school to observe and talk with children in the cafeteria and playground, and to work with them in their classrooms.

High school students will make regular visits to elementary school classrooms. These visits will be arranged by the students at the convenience of the cooperating elementary school teachers. What happens in the elementary school classroom depends in part on the teacher, what he or she would like the students to do with the children, and on the writing projects of the high school students.

Attendance Form

To: (elementary school teacher)

From: (high school teacher)

Date:

The following students have been assigned to work with your first graders. They will contact you next week to make appointments to visit your class from time to time. Please keep a record of their visits and send it to me each week, adding any comments or observations you wish to make.

Thank you for your help.

(Names of students)

Sample Thank-You Letters

Date

Elementary school teacher
Address

Dear :

My students and I thank you and your children for allowing us to use your classroom as our "laboratory" for "Kid Lit." Without your cooperation and that of the children of (name of school), we could not offer this course/unit. The stimulation of visits to your classroom encouraged my students to work particularly hard to produce stories and poems for young children.

My students want to thank the children by giving them some of the stories and poems they created. I'm enclosing a few selected pieces they hope will appeal to the children.

We plan to offer this course/unit again next year and hope you will allow us to visit your classroom. Until then, please accept our most hearty thanks for all your help this year.

Sincerely,

cc: elementary school principal
      district superintendent

Date

Elementary school principal
Address

Dear :

Thank you for allowing my high school students to visit (name of
school) and work with your children. We are very much aware that
without your cooperation and that of the staff and children of (name
of school) we could not offer this popular course/unit, "Kid Lit."
The stimulation of the visits to (name of school) and assistance of
your staff, particularly (names of cooperating teachers and librarian), encouraged my high school students to create many stories and
poems for young children. Perhaps more important than writing
for the children, my students began to remember and understand
what it is like to be little and vulnerable. Every one of my students
developed a particular affection and identity with the youngsters.
And every one of them said he or she learned a great deal about
how to relate to children. In fact, my students became very protective of their special students.

I'm sending to the children in (teachers' names) classes some of
the stories and poems my students created for them. Thank-you
notes from my students are also included.

We will offer this course again next year and hope you will continue
to allow our collaboration with your teachers and students. In the
meantime, thank you heartily for your help this year.

Sincerely,

BUYER BEWARE

ANGIE: Well, what do you feel like doing tonight?
MARTY: I don't know, Angie. What do you feel like doing?
ANGIE: Well, we ought to do something. It's Saturday night. I don't wanna
          go bowling like last Saturday. How about calling up that big girl
          we picked up inna movies about a month ago in the RKO Chester?
MARTY: I don't like her, Angie. I don't feel like calling her up.
ANGIE: Well, what do you feel like doing tonight?
MARTY: I don't know. What do you feel like doing?

(from Marty *by Paddy Chayefsky)*

Throughout our lives we must make decisions about many things, including what to do with our time, what to wear or eat, whom to choose as friends, whom to elect for public office, and what to do with our lives. Making intelligent choices is difficult for everyone, but it is especially so for teenagers. For this reason, we need to help them develop a methodology for decision making that will enable them to exert more control over their lives.

We begin by raising the consciousness of our students about the many ways their choices are influenced by outside forces, particularly the media. To help them become aware of media manipulation, we examine advertising techniques. Students look at magazine ads and bring in three they believe to be the most persuasive. In their journals they analyze the ads, determining what heightens the appeal of each, the target audience, the assumptions made about that audience, and the way in which each ad reflects these assumptions.

We divide the class into groups of three. We do this by clipping several popular advertisements selected from magazines students like to read, such as *Rolling Stone, Seventeen,* and *Sports Illustrated.* We cut each ad into three parts. The number of ads we use depends upon the class size and the number of groups we need to create. Each student reaches into a grab bag and takes one part of an ad. The groups are formed as students reassemble the ads. In their newly formed groups they review the analyses of the advertisements they have brought to class. Then they discuss each ad, looking for at least one additional technique that influences readers to buy the product. Each group chooses the most persuasive ad to present to the class.

We list on the board the various advertising techniques each group has noted. The class brainstorms on other techniques they know about to add to this list. They usually mention sex appeal, humor, catchy slogans, musical jingles, dollar value, peer approval, and snob appeal.

Students then focus on a single technique: the use of slogans. They are told that they have been hired by a company that manufactures campaign buttons. The groups are to create slogans and design buttons for a variety of student-centered purposes, such as promoting student power, eliminating homework, installing vending machines in the cafeteria—anything that is of interest to students and relevant to the school situation. The slogan must be brief, no more than five or six words, but it must also have impact. Each group presents its three best campaign buttons to the class, explaining the rationales for the slogans. Students' slogans have ranged from the banal and obvious, such as "Power to the Students" and "Homework Has to Go," to the more serious "Drive Safe, Not High" and "Give Thanks by Giving to Others."

Then we have the class work together to create an ad for a fictitious soft drink, a new, improved ginger ale targeted for the preteen audience. The class brainstorms on the adjectives they could use to describe the drink, such as: effervescent, sparkly, flavorful, refreshing, bubbly, tangy, gingery, mysterious, nippy. We encourage them to seek vivid words that appeal to all the senses. Then they decide on pictures that will appeal to their target audience.

When the ads are completed, each one is presented to the class, which then votes on the most effective one. Students discuss the reasons for their choice and what appeals most to them in the winning ad.

Now each group is ready to create an advertisement for a fictitious product of the group's invention for a particular audience, such as young mothers, senior citizens, urban professionals, or teenagers. Group members brainstorm for adjectives, appropriate to the target audience, that describe the product and appeal to the senses of taste, touch, smell, sound, and sight. They put the finished results on large posters that are displayed around the room.

Following this initial experience with ad making, we ask students to bring to class videos of popular television commercials (we keep a supply on file for emergencies) and to give an analysis of the techniques used to make them effective. The class discusses how TV commercials create the desire in us to buy products, the prejudices these ads often reveal, and the extent to which they may be sexist or elitist.

To reinforce some of the learning about the powers of media persuasion, we ask students to choose a popular TV commercial to parody. To demonstrate the process, we show a well-known TV commercial; what we select varies with what is current and popular among our students. In one demonstration we selected a commercial for Calvin Klein's fragrance Obsession in which, a beautiful, sensuous, scantily attired young woman is draped on a couch. A young man approaches her and stares at her with desire as she vanishes. Her face then fills the television screen, and she says, "In each life there is but one obsession." The last screen shows the fragrance bottle. We ask students to help us identify the techniques used by the ad-makers to sell this product. Students have no difficulty recognizing the obvious sex appeal and identification of the product with that which is exotic or unattainable and therefore all the more desirable. We point out that this is only one version of essentially the same commercial frequently shown on all channels and that the resulting viewer familiarity with the product enhances its appeal.

To model the process of creating a parody, we enlist the aid of the class to construct a comic version of this popular fragrance ad. In one of the classes, Ruth and her students developed the following parody. The opening scene is the same, with a scantily clad woman draped on a couch. But this time, as the man approaches her, he inhales her fragrance, sneezes, trips, and falls on his face. The woman puts her foot on his head, sprays him with the fragrance and says, "Take that, you chauvinist pig." His face contorts with pain and revulsion as her face then fills the screen. She says, "My life is now rid of his obsession." The lastscreen shows a bottle labeled "Obsession Repellent."

Once students have the idea of how to create a parody, they are ready to invent others. In their groups they decide which commercials to parody. They outline the original commercial on paper and determine the elements in it most susceptible to parody. Students may select a commercial from those we've shown in class or select another they have seen on television. We don't care, as long as they can identify the persuasive devices they are poking fun at to develop their "revised" commercial. Students then either videotape their parodies or present them live before the class. Presentation day is always lively and a great deal of fun. The class is filled with laughter. Students enjoy recognizing what commercials are being parodied, and they appreciate the effect of the humorous changes.

Before ending our consideration of TV commercials, we ask students to watch for those commercials that manage to persuade without appealing to prejudices or being sexist or creating false expectations in us as consumers. As a sample, we present for discussion a 30-second commercial, such as Nabisco's promotion for Teddy Grahams. In this commercial a group of children is sitting on a bench sharing a box of Teddy Grahams® snack packs. Unfortunately, the treats are so popular that the last child gets nothing but an empty box. The scene changes to show lots of children, each wearing a Teddy Graham® shirt, cheering and dancing to a catchy rock beat. The camera pans to a rooftop on which three animated animals are playing instruments and singing a tribute to the wonderfulness of Teddy Grahams®.

We then discuss what is so appealing about this commercial and encourage students to describe at least one other such ad that they find on TV. During the next class period we share the results of their research, noting how these particular commercials persuade without distorting the truth or offending anyone. Students often bring in bouncy, musical commercials, such as those produced for McDonald's, or humorous word-play commercials, such as those advertising Nut & Honey Crunch O's® cereal and any of the institutional commercials produced for General Electric. For their final project on advertising, students create full-fledged advertising/sales campaigns for the fictitious products for which they made the posters. They can use audiovisual aids, skits, songs, slogans, jingles, additional posters, whatever they think will sell their products. If possible, they create replicas of their products to show the class. Each campaign should last approximately 10–15 minutes. Students have invented products such as an automatic test taker, a flying car that folds up and can be carried a fountain-of-youth beauty tonic, a noncaloric banana split, a new movie called *The Attack of the Zealous Zucchinis,* a novel entitled *Dorinda's Desperate Days,* and multiflavored popcorn.

A useful extension of this project is to have student groups devise a way to promote a cause, e.g., persuading people to stop smoking, convincing them not to drive drunk, warning them of the dangers of casual sex, or discouraging the use of drugs. A major part of the groups' work involves the creation of a skit to be videotaped, convincing an audience of the validity of their cause. Each group also presents a vivid poster for its cause. Groups then visit one or two other classes and present the results of their efforts. Evaluation forms (see Addendum) are completed by members of the other classes, indicating what was most persuasive in each presentation and what needed more emphasis. Students then meet in their groups to discuss the evaluations.

For these activities, as with earlier projects in this unit, we face the necessity of providing grades. This task is made easier by engaging our students early on to determine the criteria for success of each project. Together we identify the following criteria for determining the project's group grade:

- Originality of ideas
- Evidence of careful analysis
- Appropriateness of audience appeals
- Attention to detail
- Attractiveness of product
- Persuasiveness of appeal

In grading the group project, we recognize that some students contribute more than others. However, giving a group grade encourages responsibility in each member for the success of the project, thus promoting cooperation and interdependence. Nevertheless, because there often is a disparity of effort within the group, some students resist having only a group grade. We have overcome this by also giving each student an individual grade based on our assessment of his or her contribution to the group project.

So far in this unit students have learned to recognize the many ways in which we as consumers are influenced by advertising to favor one product over another. They should now be able to be more discerning in their choices of products. Many of these same advertising techniques are used to distort other messages we receive. To help students become more informed citizens and to distinguish propaganda from objective presentation of facts, we have students study the newspapers to discover how seemingly objective reporting can distort their perceptions of an event. Students are given the following two accounts of an accident:

> On Monday afternoon an accident occurred on the Taconic Parkway. Sixteen-year-old Jeffrey Wills of Katonah crossed the median barrier and entered the opposite lane, crashing into the side of an oncoming car. The two females in the other car sustained minor injuries. Traffic was slowed briefly, but the two cars were removed before rush hour. Mr. Wills was given a summons for reckless driving.
>
> On Monday afternoon, there was a two-car collision on the Taconic Parkway. A car speeding at 90 miles an hour and driven by 16-year-old

Jeffrey Wills, an unlicensed high school dropout from Katonah, careened out of control, crossing the median barrier and entering the opposite lane, crashing into the side of an oncoming vehicle. Fortunately, the 65-year-old grandmother and her 5-year-old grandchild sustained only minor injuries. However, both cars were severely damaged and had to be towed away to allow the rush hour traffic to proceed normally. Traffic was backed up for three miles as a result of the accident. Mr. Wills was given a summons for driving while intoxicated and for driving without a license. This accident is just one more example of an increasing trend in our community for young drivers to endanger themselves and others by reckless and drunken driving.

The class examines these two accounts of the same event and note the differences. Students discuss the attitude apparent in the second account and the bias-laden elements in it, seeking to establish the ways in which we are led to be prejudiced not only against the young male driver but in fact all young male drivers. Some they mention are:

- Slanted perspective
- Emotion-charged language
- Selection of details (grandmother and grandchild, reckless, drunken, high school dropout)
- Personal evaluation at the end

Students are then divided into groups of three to examine differing accounts of a single event. We determine the group membership to ensure heterogeneity of ability. Students may use regional, local, and national publications such as *U.S.A. Today, The Wall Street Journal, The Christian Science Monitor, The Nation, The New Republic, U.S. News and World Report, Time,* and *Newsweek.* We encourage our students to find as many different reports of the event as possible, but they'll need at least two, obviously. They analyze the reports, looking for differences:

- What is left out?
- What is added?
- How do the changes affect the perceptions they have of that event?
- What bias, if any, do they discover in each account?
- Do they note any racial, ethnic, gender, class, or political bias?

Each group presents its findings to the class and shares the articles.

As a further extension of this activity, student groups are sent to observe various locations in the school: the cafeteria, gym, dean's office, library, and student gathering places inside and outside the building. They keep journals of what they see and hear. They observe during lunch hour and between classes. When they return to class, they discuss what they have observed. They select the most newsworthy event, such as a confrontation between students or between a staff member and a student. Occasionally we have staged such confrontations in the absence of any real-life models, but most of the time there are all too many examples from which to draw. Students list all the details of the event from notes they take at the scene and from memory. They then seek out witnesses to interview and get materials relevant to the incident.

Once the information has been collected, we direct each group to assume a different persona and write an account of the event for the school newspaper. We put several choices of personae in a hat and have each group select one. Possibilities include a strict administrator, the superintendent, a liberal teacher, a male student witness, a friend of one of the parties to the incident, a female student witness, friend of the alleged instigator of the incident, a student who did not see the incident but is very concerned about the school disciplinary climate, a student rebel, an elderly community resident who happened to be in the building at the time, and a member of the school board. Choices of personae will depend on the nature of the incident students will develop into an article. The resulting articles are photocopied and examined by the class to see how each group handled the facts and yet reflected the bias of the persona.

Ruth staged an incident in which one student (unbeknownst to her classmates) agreed to impersonate a student accused of driving recklessly past a school bus. The assistant principal played the role of an overwrought administrator. After the "incident," enacted in the classroom, students chose a persona from whose perspective they wrote reports of the incident. Kathy and her group assumed the persona of the accused:

> I can't believe Mr. Maher did that! He just barged into the classroom and started accusing me of almost killing some little kid in front of the middle school. He didn't care about my feelings but just started shouting at me in front of the whole class. I was not even driving at that time; I was in class. Just because someone saw my car doesn't mean that I did it. Someone else had borrowed my car yesterday morning. Did he ever think of that? No— he just accused me in front of everyone. I feel so embarrasssed and I didn't even do anything to deserve that. He could have asked me calmly—and in private. I can't believe he had the nerve to embarrass me like that. He never thought what I would feel like being accused of something as horrible as that! I know people are saying things behind my back. A couple of people have even made nasty comments to my face—and they don't even know the whole story.

Ray and his group wrote about the incident as an observer:

> It was fifth period. I was sitting in English class, relaxing after my hectic morning. I had had to borrow a friend's car in order to get to school. Even still, I did not get in until a quarter to nine and was dodging the dean who I was sure would be after me.
>
> Then there was a knock on the door of the classroom. My teacher opened it. I looked up and saw the dean walk in, talking in a low voice to the teacher. My heart raced. I looked down so as not to attract attention. I heard

the dean say, "I just have to speak to one student." He walked across the room to the side on which I sat. I began to anticipate what I would say. The dean walked towards me and then right past me. He was not looking at me at all but went to Michelle (the friend whose car I borrowed). He started talking to Michelle quietly. I strained to hear but could not.

After a few words, Michelle said loudly, "I was here 2nd period." The dean raised his voice to the level of hers.

"Then where did you park?"

"In the commuter lot," she responded.

"Were you in homeroom?"

"Yes," she snarled.

"Were you or were you not driving your car around eight thirty this morning?"

"No," she said loudly.

My heart beat even faster. My friend was being accused of doing something I did.

"There were people who said they saw you drive past that bus. They said you didn't stop and nearly hit a kid getting off."

"That's not true."

"Didn't you drive in late this morning?" he barked.

"No!" she said emphatically.

"Yes or no?" he asked, ignoring her answer.

"No!"

"Well, people said they saw you driving past the middle school very fast. You didn't stop for the bus."

"But I . . ."

"You almost killed that kid."

"It wasn't me. I lent my car to someone."

"Who?"

"I can't tell you."

"You lent your car to someone to drive to school?"

"Yes."

The dean paused, seeing that this interrogation was going nowhere. "Well, people say they saw you, and I have a screaming parent in my office." Then, to the teacher: "I'm sorry, I'm going to have to take her to the office." Then, to Michelle: "Get your books."

Michelle got up and pushed the desk out of her way contemptuously. She glanced at me for a second before being nearly shoved out the door.

Sara and her group assumed the persona of the victim:

It started out to be a normal day. I got up a little late, so I rushed through my shower, threw on my favorite jeans and Albany sweatshirt. Quickly I scattered for my books and shoved them in my book bag. I grabbed a waffle as I ran out the door, almost forgetting my Redskins hat. I made it to the bus stop just in time. I threw myself in my seat and adjusted my hat.

Suddenly, David Johnson, an 8th grader, came up to me, grabbed my hat and screamed, "Monkey in the middle!" I struggled to get it back, but almost everyone was enjoying the game with me being the monkey.

As the bus pulled up to the school, Kenny Niles threw my hat out the window. I ran out in front of the bus and into the street to get it. Suddenly, a car came to a screeching stop an inch away from me. I fell to the ground and sat there in complete shock, while the car quickly worked its way around me and sped off.

I didn't really see the car or the driver because I was too frightened. I just remember it was big and white. Teachers and students ran up to me. Dr. Sieverding asked me, "Are you all right, are you hurt? Quick, someone, get the nurse."

I paused for a bit, then pushed myself off the ground and responded, "No, I'm okay, just had the wind knocked out of me."

"Don't worry, son," someone said. "We got the license plate. It must have been a high school student. Let's go call your mom."

He walked me to the nurse and then went back to his office. Ten minutes went by with me counting the squares on the ceiling. Nothing was really wrong with me; I was just a little shaken up, but the nurse was sure to inspect every part of my body anyway. I guess it gave her something to do.

Suddenly I heard the door slam open. "Where is he? Where's my baby?"

Oh great, I thought, my neurotic mother. The nurse tried to calm her down. "Mrs. Thomas, Jonathan is just fine. No cuts or bruises, just. . ."

Ignoring her, my mother ran in to me, "Johnny, my poor baby. Are you all right?"

"Yeah, mom, I'm fine," I said.

"Don't worry, honey, we're going to find that mean, nasty driver and make him pay for your pain and anguish."

"Mom, really, that's okay, I'm fine." She still wasn't listening. "I'm going over to the high school right now. They think they know who the driver is. You rest tight, sweetheart, and mommy will fix everything."

She rushed out before I could stop her. I really didn't want that person to get in trouble. I mean, it was mostly my fault. I did run out into the street. Well, I'll get everything straightened out tomorrow. Right now I think I'll go to sleep and just be happy that I don't have to take my math test.

Because we wanted to contrast the persona reports of the incident with a more objective version, we invited a reporter for the school newspaper to interview the various people connected with the incident. He wrote this account:

On May 1 during Mrs. Townsend's fifth period English class, Mr. Wally Maher, Dean of Discipline, interrupted class to accuse Michelle DiMarco of driving recklessly past a stopped middle school bus at 8:30 am and almost running over Jonathan Thomas who was attempting to disembark. Before Mr. Maher could persuade Michelle to come with him to the office, a loud argument between them erupted. The rest of the class reacted in stunned silence.

Mr. Maher said he had reliable witnesses who saw Michelle fail to stop for the bus. They reported that her big white car was going well over the 10 mph limit and didn't stop even after Jonathan Thomas fell to the ground. Mr. Sieverding, the Assistant Principal at the middle school, got the license plate number from a student who had written it down at the time of the incident. That number checked out as belonging to Michelle DiMarco's car. When questioned about his action, Mr. Maher said, "It was my job to investigate the incident and discipline Michelle if she was the guilty party. Her account was inconsistent. First, she said she had parked her car in the commuter parking lot. Then she said she had lent it to a friend the day before. She got defensive and hostile. Ordinarily I would have taken her out of the classroom before questioning her, but she was very defiant and started arguing with me before I could remove her from the class."

Michelle claims she is innocent. She says she was in homeroom during the time she is accused of having driven past the stopped school bus. According to her, she had lent the car to a friend the day before and wasn't even driving it that morning. She is furious that she was humiliated in front of her friends in Mrs. Townsend's class. She said, "He had no right to barge in there and yell at me like that in front of everybody. He had no real evidence that I was driving the car. Why couldn't he just have quietly asked me to come to the office with him. Then I could have explained to him what really happened."

Jonathan Thomas was shaken up but not injured in the incident. Mrs. Thomas, however, is not satisfied with the school's handling of the incident. She said, "I don't understand what students are doing roaming around the parking lot in their cars well after school starts. What kind of school is it anyway? I intend to press charges against Miss DiMarco for reckless driving and failure to stop for a school bus. I may sue the school as well for negligence."

Mrs. Townsend refused to comment on the incident beyond saying that Mr. Maher was acting properly in his capacity as dean of discipline. Once Michelle and Mr. Maher had left, she used the interruption as a writing opportunity and had her students write their observations in their journals.

As a class we review these reports and identify the biases and prejudices in those written by people involved in one way or another in the incident. We contrast the persona reports with that of the school newspaper reporter assigned to cover the incident. We note his focus on the Dean's intrusion into the classroom, the objectivity with which he reports what happened, and his presentation of both sides through his interviews with the dean and with Michelle. We point out the critical necessity for news to be reported objectively and the ease with which writers can influence the thinking of their readers by the details they choose to include.

Next, we examine editorials in which subjective writing is acceptable. Students bring to class editorials from the local newspaper (we also keep an assortment of current pieces on hand) and comment in their journals on methods of persuasion used in the editorials. They ask themselves:

- What is the point of the editorial?
- Is it biased?
- Does it present more than one side of an issue?
- What questions does it raise?
- What devices does the author use to convince the audience to accept the point of view of the editorial?

At this point, depending upon the literature being studied by the class, students are assigned the task of writing a persuasive editorial about one of the characters in their literature. For example, they may defend or attack George's killing of Lennie in *Of Mice And Men*, argue for or against Gene in *A Separate Peace*, persuade an audience that Kino in *The Pearl* was right or wrong to throw away the pearl at the end, argue for or against inclusion of *Inherit the Wind* or *Huckleberry Finn* or *Catcher in the Rye* in the school curriculum.

Kristen wrote this defense of *Catcher in the Rye* to a California town school board that had prohibited classroom use of Salinger's book:

Ladies and Gentlemen:
I am writing to you about your decision banning the book *Catcher in the Rye* in your high school. I was very upset when I read about this action in *The New York Times*.

This book should not be banned. In fact, it should be put back into the curriculum. I believe this because Holden Caulfield, the main character, is a heroic person, a protector of children and an unselfish helper of others.

Holden is a heroic person and a protector of children because he cares very much about them and wants to be the "catcher in the rye," the savior of innocent little kids from all the corrupt things in the world. He says he wants "to catch everybody if they start to go over the cliff—I mean if they're running and they don't look where they're going. I have to go somewhere and catch them. That's all I'd do all day. I know it's crazy, but that's the only thing I'd really like to be."

Holden is unselfish towards others; he puts their needs in front of himself. One time Holden wrote a hundred page composition for his roommate, Stradlater, so he wouldn't fail. And he also lent his typewriter to one of his dormmates, but what Holden mostly cared about was his sister, Phoebe. "You ought to see old Phoebe," he said, "she has this sort of red hair, a little bit like Allie's was, that's very short in the summertime. In the summertime she sticks it behind her ears. She has nice pretty little ears. She's quite skinny, like me, but nice skinny. Roller skate skinny. I watched from my window roller skating in the park and that's what she is, roller skate skinny. You'd like her."

Holden is like a lot of teenagers who have problems and feel like they just want to get away from it all. This book will help them understand more about people. At least, I know the students at my high school learned a lot from it. *Catcher in the Rye* is not just one of those boring books you have to read in English class; it's a book that will keep students interested because no matter where they live they can relate to it. They can really understand when Holden says, "Did you ever get fed up? I mean did you ever get scared that everything was going to go lousy unless you did something?"

I really think you should reconsider the banning of this book. I recommend it to everyone, and I think it should be put back into your curriculum.

An engaging and relevant extension of the entire unit involves a full-fledged election campaign. Many books lend themselves to this activity. For example, students can choose a leader for the group of boys in Golding's *Lord of the Flies*, or they can campaign for head of state in Shakespeare's *Macbeth* or *Julius Ceasar*. This activity has the advantage of giving students the opportunity to be creative as they use the techniques of persuasion studied in the other activities in the unit. Perhaps more important, though, an election helps students learn to be involved, productive citizens who understand the process of political campaigning.

In this activity they practice arguing persuasively, making decisions based on real issues, differentiating propaganda from argumentation, and presenting their ideas orally and in writing to a real audience, their peers. In addition, because they base their campaigns on their knowledge of literature they have read, they gain skill in analysis of character. In order to run an effective campaign for their candidates, students must analyze the personalities of the characters in the literature in some depth. Perhaps most significant, an election campaign has built-in interest for students as they respond enthusiastically to the element of competition and the opportunity to engage in an activity they recognize as "real."

Shakespeare's *Julius Ceasar* lends itself particularly well to an election campaign, which certainly provides the motivation to review the characteristics of the protagonists. Because students often seem mystified by Shakespeare's language and have great difficulty following the play even as we act it out, the campaign enables students to become comfortable with the text in ways impossible with traditional study questions and tests. It also gives us the opportunity to engage them in writing for and speaking to a live audience.

We begin by dividing the class into groups of four, carefully structuring each group so that it contains at least one student who has demonstrated some understanding of Shakespeare's language, is willing to express ideas orally, and, most important, can function as a leader for the group. Those students less able academically we distribute among the various class groups so that no one group has an obvious advantage over another.

Students determine which characters could be potential candidates for Emperor of Rome. From among the major characters—Caesar, Brutus, Antony, Cassius, Octavius, and Portia—each group is assigned one candidate to promote. The selection of candidates is accomplished by placing all the names in a grab bag and having a member of each group reach in and select one name. Once every group has a candidate, the group members' task is to conduct an effective campaign to get their candidate elected Emperor of Rome. Each group elects a chairperson and designates a recorder. Groups give themselves names such as The Brutes, The Flying Buttresses, and The Octavians.

Before getting involved in group work, the class brainstorms, drawing on students' knowledge of real elections. Then each group plans the strategy of its campaign, dividing the work among the members. Students decide on the campaign materials they will create: posters, banners, newsletters, mottoes, videos, TV commercials, caricatures, and even gift pencils and lollipops. Each group is charged with having at least one part of the campaign completed for the next class day as a kickoff for the campaign. In addition, a member of each group prepares a speech nominating his or her group's candidate.

In a tenth-grade class recently, Marcia was astonished to see how much her students had accomplished in one day. Before class began, students began decorating the room with posters and campaign banners. One group brought in a huge banner reading "Elect Caesar; He's No Geezer." Another made a poster with a rising sun advertising Brutus. Still another had written a rap song promoting Cassius. One group, in addition to having created a poster and buttons advertising its candidate, handed out pencils with the candidate's name etched on them. Each group presented its efforts and nominated its candidate, thus launching the election campaign.

In succeeding days students brought in more posters, banners, and campaign gimmicks to promote their candidates. The project generated more enthusiasm and excitement than Marcia had expected. The election took on a life of its own, to which she as the teacher became a mere spectator. Her room was literally redecorated from floor to ceiling with campaign literature, which even spilled over into other classrooms and the halls.

Once students have launched their candidates, we generate a focused review of *Julius Caesar* by structuring each day's claswork for the groups. The first day involves reviewing the play for all the positive things that can be said about the candidates. Students find specific references to support all the positive comments they wish to make on behalf of their candidates. The next day they review the play, looking for all the negative references to the opposition candidates. In so doing, they recognize the genesis of the negative campaigning in vogue today.

Each group keeps a portfolio of all its accumulated campaign literature. We tell the groups they will be judged by the quality of their portfolios, which include all they have written: newsletters, letters of endorsement for their candidates, commercials, and editorials. On the last day of the campaign, they help their candidates compose opening speeches and write questions to ask the other candidates during a debate—the climax of the campaign.

On debate day students usually arrive in class very excited. Some don togas and preen for the video camera set up to record the event, which is performed for an invited audience of students from other classes and an assortment of teachers and administrators who act as judges.

The candidates pick numbers out of a hat for positions in the debate. Each opening speech is two to three minutes long and meant to be impressive. Students are usually well prepared and reveal considerable knowledge of the play. For example, in one class, "Caesar" said:

> Fellow Romans, we are gathered here today to choose once and for all a leader for our beloved Rome. This is not a decision you should take lightly. Before you stand six candidates, one of whom has no credentials, two of whom are murderers, another who promotes riots, and one other young, inexperienced boy, and finally, I, his uncle, a supported, effective and

proven leader. . . . I am ready to lead Rome now; in fact, I had been doing so for a while and did so well that I was offered the crown by the Senate. I was raised to be a leader. I was well schooled and have proven myself as a strong leader many times. My armies added huge expanses to the empire, bringing riches to the people of Rome. Not just the rich, mind you, but the poor as well. They were provided with bread and circuses, and I redistributed land to them. . . . It is easy to see that I, Julius Caesar, am the ideal choice. I have more qual-ifications and experience than the others, and I care deeply for you, the people. Rome should not have to settle for less than the BEST.

Each of the candidates gives a speech that reflects the seriousness with which the students tackle this debate. The debaters are very competitive, and each is eager to outshine the others. After the opening speeches, students ask candidates incisive questions, such as:

■ "Antony, if you care so much about the people, why did you risk your servant's life to find out if it was safe for you to meet with the conspirators?"
   or
"Brutus, if you are so loyal, why did you betray Caesar? How can we be sure you won't betray us as well?"
   or
"Caesar, if you believe you can't do anything wrong, then how can we be sure we will still have a voice in the government once you have been elected?"

After the question-and-answer session, each candidate gives a closing speech, reaffirming his or her fine qualities of leadership and asking for the support of the people of Rome. Judges have ballots on which they rate each of the candidates on a scale of 1 to 10 for presentation, content, and the ability to field questions. Opening and closing speeches are rated separately.

Excitement about the campaign does not immediately dissipate; students are always eager to know who has won the debate and the election. To the winners we award certificates and prizes of pens or key rings.

The election campaign not only captivates students' interest but involves them in a total language experience: They read, process what they read, write about what they know and about what they think, synthesize data, evaluate performance, speak before an audience, and work collaboratively to learn from each other. The following excerpt from Alex's journal reflects the generally positive response to the campaign:

■ *Julius Caesar* was an interesting play. I liked how Shakespeare added to the historical characters. It was more fun reading it than learning about this period in Social Studies. The campaign we had afterwards was great. I liked being able to do something with what we read, not just forgetting about it. I learned more that way than I would have by just reading it. I was also glad that my group won for the best campaign because I put a lot of effort into it.

The activities of the election campaign have immediate implications when we time them to coincide with local or national political campaigns. We encourage our students to take an active part in the political process, practicing what they have learned about developing persuasive arguments, differentiating between fact and opinion, recognizing the techniques of propaganda, and using their speaking and writing skills to influence the outcome of community events.

Like Marty and Angie in Paddy Chayefsky's play, disenchanted students often don't know what they want to do or where they want to go, much less what they believe. But when they have an opportunity to work independently and collaboratively, be creative, and see the successful results of their thoughtful decision making, such as those generated by the advertising and election campaigns, they can understand the relevance of their work and respond positively to the immediate rewards they receive for it.

For us as teachers, these activities involve risktaking, tolerance for more than the usual noise in a classroom, and a willingness to let students take responsibility for their own learning. However, these are the only conditions in which real learning for any of us ever takes place.

A SPORTING LIFE

Caught off first, he leaped to run to second, but
Then struggled back to first.
He left first because of a natural desire
To leap, to get on with the game.
When you jerk to run to second
You do not necessarily think of a home run.
You want to go on. You want to get to the next stage,
The entire soul is bent on second base.
The fact is that the mind flashes
Faster in action than the muscles can move
Dramatic! Off first, taut, heading for second,
In a split second, total realization,
Heading for first. Head first! Legs follow fast
You struggle back to first with victor effort
As, even, after a life of effort and chill,
One flashes back to the safety of childhood,
To that strange place where one had first begun.
             "Ball Game" by Richard Eberhart.

Even the most apathetic of our students responds to the challenge of competition, especially athletic competition. In fact, our students love sports. They love playing sports, watching sports, thinking about sports, discussing sports. For many of them playing on school teams or in intramurals, their "entire soul is bent on second." By constructing a language and literature unit around this intense interest, we engage them easily and totally.

We begin by adapting a favorite icebreaker to our sports theme. Each student is given a sheet of names of all-time sports greats. The sheet is divided into 25 boxes with one name per box. Students are instructed to write down what they know about as many sports stars as they can identify. The first one to complete the sheet wins. Students circulate around the room, trying to learn about sports stars unfamiliar to them in order to complete their sheets. This activity is a lot of fun and encourages active participation by all students. Some of the names we have used successfully are Babe Ruth, Althea Gibson, Joe Dimaggio, Magic Johnson, Michael Jordan, Martina Navratalova, Pete Rose, Arthur Ashe, Henry Aaron, Jackie Robinson, Evelyn Ashford, Rosie Greer, and Bo Jackson. Students themselves are a good source for names. Sometimes we have one group of students prepare the sheet for another group of students. We try to select names of people who have made major contributions to their sports and who have had to overcome personal and professional obstacles in order to achieve their full potential.

Once the winner of the icebreaker has been determined, we process this activity, discussing the contributions of each person on the sheet. Students then select one sports star to research. We make sure that each student selects a different person. If someone has a burning desire to study a star not on the original list, we try to be flexible enough to accommodate her or him. As a class, we brainstorm the kinds of questions students should consider in their study of their sports star. Students have suggested such questions as:

■ What made him or her an outstanding athlete?
■ What obstacles did he or she have to overcome?
■ What contribution did she or he make to the game and to the world at large?

We tell our students that when they find the answers to these questions, they should record them in research notebooks, which they may store in class for safekeeping. Then we take them to the library for an orientation session. This is the first encounter with the library for many of our disenchanted students. Prior to the visit, we arrange with the librarian to tell our students how to find materials in the library. He shows them the resources of the library, including the card catalog, TOMS, the *Guide to Periodical Literature,* and the computer connection with the county library system. Following the orientation, we help them use these resources to look for information about their sports star in newspaper articles, in magazines, and in full-length biographies. We give students one week to complete this research. While they are working on their own sports star, we also gather data on a sports figure who interests us—for instance, Althea Gibson.

We tell the students that they are going to assume the persona of their sports star, who will be interviewed by Oprah Winfrey or Geraldo Rivera and the studio audience. These interviews will be videotaped. To help them prepare, we model the process of organizing the collected data into categories. With the overhead projector, we display the raw data we have collected on Althea Gibson. The students can see that the information falls into several distinct categories, such as personal background, obstacles, accomplishments, attitudes, and influence on others. We rearrange our data so it fits into these categories. We put the details from each category on separate 5-by-8-inch index cards. Our next step is to select the student who will assume the persona of Oprah or Geraldo. Usually this is a pop-ular role to play. If more than one student is eager to do it, we hold an audition, asking the student to demonstrate how he or she will personify Geraldo or Oprah. Then we let the class vote. If no one volunteers, a rare occurrence, we have to assign the role to a student who we believe will be successful in this role. In either event, we prime our Geraldo/Oprah to ask questions relating to each category, making sure each sports figure has an opportunity to respond to each question. This means the student has to be conscious of time and not allow one person to dominate the conversation.

While we are working with Geraldo/Oprah, students practice playing their roles. They will be interviewed in groups of five to enable each student-impersonator to have enough time to talk about him- or herself.

On the day of the presentations we set up the videocamera and enlist the assistance of a student. Because so many of our students have experience with comcorders at school or at home, it is easy to find someone to help us.

To begin, Geraldo/Oprah introduces the "guests" and begins the questioning. The moderator invites the audience to ask questions that relate to what has already been discussed. On the first day or two we often have to intercede to help keep track of the limited time available. Students always respond positively to this activity and find that oral presentation in this context is nonthreatening and fun.

We evaluate the presentations based on how well students seem to know their person and on the thoroughness of the notes they took in their research notebooks.

After the presentations are completed, we talk about the popularity of sports in our society. Some of our best writers have been inspired by their love of sports to write novels, short stories, plays, even poetry. We look at some of the poetry written about sports, beginning with Eberhart's "Ball Game," with which we began this chapter. We ask which students particularly love to play baseball. Usually several students respond. We then ask one of them to read Eberhart's poem aloud and another one to act it out. We encourage the class to offer suggestions on how best to portray the action in the poem. Students enjoy this dramatic portrayal of a scene they recognize very well, a struggle to steal a base and then the flying leap back to the safety of the original base. We tell them to record their reactions to the poem in their notebooks. We suggest that they explain how the poet enables us to visualize the action. Invariably they identify the vivid verbs, such as "leaped," "struggled," and "jerk"—words that create pictures of motion. We ask them why these particular verbs work so well in this context. They tell us that these words accurately and precisely depict the actions in baseball.

We also ask them to comment on the connection the poet makes between running the bases in baseball and growing up. They usually see each base as a metaphor for a stage in life. From this discussion, students begin to understand the metaphor of the failed stolen base as the retreat to the safety of childhood, and they often question the validity of that analogy. To them, childhood does not necessarily represent safety from a life "of effort and chill," especially not to the disenchanted, who often have had difficult childhood experiences.

As the next stage in our study of the poetry of sports, students are randomly assigned into groups of three and given a poem to read, one rich in imagery — such as "Ex-Basketball Player" by John Updike:

> Pearl Avenue runs past the high-school lot,
> Bends with the trolley tracks, and stops, cut off
> Before it has a chance to go two blocks,
> At Colonel McComsky Plaza. Berth's Garage
> Is on the corner facing west, and there,
> Most days, you'll find Flick Webb, who helps Berth out.

Flick stands tall among the idiot pumps—
Five on a side, the old bubble-head style,
Their rubber elbows hanging loose and low.
One's nostrils are two S's, and his eyes
An E and O. And one is squat, without
A head at all—more of a football type.

Once Flick played for the high-school team, the Wizards.
He was good: in fact, the best. In '46
He bucketed three hundred ninety points,
A county record still. The ball loved Flick.
I saw him rack up thirty-eight or forty
In one home game. His hands were like wild birds.

He never learned a trade, he just sells gas,
Checks oil, and changes flats. Once in a while,
As a gag, he dribbles an inner tube,
But most of us remember anyway.
His hands are fine and nervous on the lug wrench.
It makes no difference to the lug wrench, though.

Off work, he hangs around Mae's Luncheonette.
Grease-grey and kind of coiled, he plays pinball,
Sips lemon cokes, and smokes those thin cigars;
Flick seldom speaks to Mae, just sits and nods
Beyond her face towards bright applauding tiers
Of Necco Wafers, Nibs, and Juju Beads.

Each student has a copy of the poem, and one student in each group reads the poem aloud to the others. A second student records stanza by stanza what the group visualizes from the language of the poem, and a third translates the verbal pictures into illustrations. We assure our students that they don't have to be artistic to illustrate the poem; stick figures and line drawings will do. Our purpose is to help them focus on Updike's words and to appreciate the vivid imagery of the poem. This assignment permits the more artistic students, some of whom often have difficulty with language-based assignments, to make a significant contribution to the reading and understanding of the poem. One such student in Marcia's class created cartoons for each stanza in order to dramatize the story of Flick's life.

As part of each group's examination of this poem, students consider the personification of the gas pumps as a basketball team and the "applauding tiers/ Of Necco Wafers, Nibs, and Juju Beads" as enthralled fans. They also talk about how the poem makes them feel about professional sports as a career aspiration for high school athletic stars. After the students have completed their consideration of the poem, a representative from each group shares the group's illustrations with the class and explains the meaning of the poem depicted by those illustrations.

These presentations launch a class discussion of students' feelings about the poem and its pessimistic appraisal of the chances for athletic success of students beyond high school. This usually leads to a lively debate. Some students become upset at Updike's implication that they are wasting their time and their chance to be somebody in life if they limit themselves to trying to become professional athletes. Others cite statistics to support Updike's view. Student involvement in the debate generated by this poem is often passionate; everyone has an opinion.

Students also raise the issue of what is success and debate the effect of popularity and fame on student athletes' later lives. Some argue that outstanding student athletes develop such positive self-images that they have better chances to be successful in anything they try in life; others argue that so much early success can spoil student athletes for anything later that fails to provide the same level of recognition. Regardless of the direction in which the discussion goes, we take this opportunity to remind students to be realistic in their aspirations to become professional athletes; the number of positions available in all sports is very small in comparison with the number of students who excel in high school athletics and hope to succeed professionally.

Our discussion of the ephemeral nature of fame prepares our students to examine "To an Athlete Dying Young" by A. E. Housman.

The time you won your town the race
We chaired you through the market place;
Man and boy stood cheering by,
And home we brought you shoulder-high.

Today, the road all runners come,
Shoulder-high we bring you home,
And set you at your threshold down,
Townsman of a stiller town.

Smart lad, to slip betimes away
From fields where glory does not stay
And early though the laurel grows
It withers quicker than the rose.

Eyes the shady night has shut
Cannot see the record cut,
And silence sounds no worse than cheers
After earth has stopped the ears.

Now you will not swell the rout
Of lads that wore their honors out,
Runners whom renown outran
And the name died before the man.

So set, before the echoes fade,
The fleet foot on the sill of shade,
And hold go the low lintel up
The still-defended challenge-cup.

And round that early-laureled head
Will flock to gaze the strengthless dead,
And find unwithered on its curls
The garland briefer than a girl's.

In this poem students need to visualize the universal context for the metaphor of a runner on the "road all runners come." Students work in the same groups of three but switch roles, with one student reading the poem, one recording group responses to it, and the third dramatizing the group's reading through a series of illustrations. We then ask students to paraphrase the poem quatrain by quatrain. We find that students need considerable assistance understanding the extended metaphor in this poem. We circulate from group to group, facilitating their discussion and helping them see the relationship between the death of the young athlete and the general problem of fame being short-lived. They may also need help recognizing the poet's ironic comment on fame and the tragedy of achievements withering "quicker than the rose." Often students reading the poem very literally get upset with Housman because they believe he is happy that the poor young athlete died so young. We need to help them recognize Housman's irony in seeming to celebrate the death of a young athlete.

When groups have had enough time to develop their illustrations and react to the poem, they share their results with the rest of the class. We display their illustrations on the bulletin board and encourage them to discuss their own feelings about whether sports should be viewed as a shortcut to fame, glory, and riches.

By this time students are comfortable with visually representing the imagery in a poem and are ready for the next activity. We give them copies of the following poems: "Casey at the Bat" by Ernest Thayer, "The Passer" by George Abbe, "A Snapshot for Miss Bricka" by Robert Wallace, "A Public Nuisance" by Reginald Arkell, "Ode to a Used Optic Yellow Wilson" by Carol Nagy, "Ballad of a Ballgame" by Christine Lavin, "In the Pocket" by James Dickey, "The Base Stealer" by Robert Francis, and "Jump Shot" by Richard Peck. We ask the librarian to collect books of contemporary poems for our students to peruse to find additional sports poems.

In their groups of three, students read a number of poems and decide on one they want to study in depth to transform into a series of visual images for a poetry video. We guide them in their selection of a poem to make sure each group has a different poem, one rich in visual imagery. We ask each group member to play a key role in determining the meaning of the poem. One student leads the group in a discussion of the dominant images. The second records the images created by the language of the poem. The third student leads the group in a discussion of the ways those images combine to reveal the speaker's attitude towards the subject. Sometimes our students are able to recognize that the speaker is different from the poet and therefore, that the attitude of the speaker may be different from that of the poet. This perception requires a sensitivity to the language on the part of the readers, but their careful attention to the words and imagery of the poem often facilitates this kind of analysis. Based on their discoveries, students reach a consensus on the meaning of the poem. We meet with each group to review its understanding and to offer help when necessary.

Once students feel comfortable with the poem, they decide how best to present it as a poetry video. To get them started, we show them student poetry videos from other classes, taking care not to present any of the poems they are considering. (The first time we used this approach, we showed music videos because, similar to the videos we want our students to produce, the performers visually enact the lyrics of their songs.) We identify the techniques used in the samples to depict the meaning in the poems through both images and music.

As part of their preparatory work on the poems, students must come to a group consensus on the best way to re-create each image in the poem they have selected, on the props to be used, the background music to include, and the actions necessary to dramatize the poem. The student in each group who acts as a recorder then begins to create the storyboard.

Evan's storyboard for Simon and Garfunkel's "The Boxer" looked like this:

What will appear on screen	Description of shots	Audio (lines of poem on screen)
		Music of Simon and Garfunkel singing "The Boxer"
A boy walks, hands in pockets, head down, listless, kicks the dust, shakes his head.	WS CU	I am just a poor boy though my story's seldom told./I have squandered my resistance for a pocket full of mumbles. Such are promises. All lies and jests.
Suddenly smiles, shrugs, walks off proudly.	MCU	Still a man hears what he wants to hear and disregards the rest
Film clips of city streets, tenements, littered parks, winos, clumps of people hanging out on street corners.	EWS	(*musical chorus*)

What will appear on screen	Description of shots	Audio (lines of poem on screen)
Film clips of lush farmland, elegant white farmhouse, small well-dressed boy carrying huge teddy bear, running down long, lonely road, pulling out a wad of bills to buy a first-class train ticket. Porters, engineers, trainmen all treat him with care.	WS CU	When I left my home and my family, I was no more than a boy/in the company of strangers, in the quiet of the railway station running scared.
Film clips of slum area: four tattered men, leaning against a boarded-up building, drinking wine out of a paper bag, city streets, homeless people building a fire to keep warm.	EWS	Laying low, seeking out the poorer quarters where the ragged people go looking for the places only they would know.

(he soon becomes disillusioned with the city and decides to go home)

Boy knocked down by two others, left crying on the ground. Dressed in old cut-offs, picks himself up, dusts off his pants, stands very tall, looks around slowly, then picks up his school bag, slings it over his shoulder and walks purposefully off toward bus depot, heading south.	MCU	In the clearing stands a boxer and a fighter by his trade, /and he carries the reminders of every glove that laid him down/or cut him till he cried out in his anger and his shame. I am leaving, I am leaving, but the fighter still remains.

Notice that the storyboard includes directions to the camera person of the kinds of shots—closeups (CU), wide-angle shot (WS), etc. (see Addendum, page 105)—that are appropriate for each stage of the poetry video, as well as the music for each section of the poem. Usually one student assumes the responsibility for determining the kinds of shots, another the illustrations of each scene, and another the lines of the poem that go with each particular scene and the appropriate background music for that scene. We always insist on approving the storyboard before students proceed with the project, but we recognize that plans may change as the actual filming gets underway. The success of the actual videotaping depends upon the practicality and detail of the storyboard, so we make suggestions for realistic ways to adapt what they already have to the demands of video. We also try to make certain that students have made appropriate visual and musical choices so that the imagery of the poem comes alive for the audience.

This stage of the project generates a great deal of excitement; students can't wait to videotape their poems. However, they need considerable rehearsal time so that they are "camera-ready" when they actually film their interpretations. We allow several class periods for students to prepare for the videotaping of their poems.

Most groups have one student read the poem while the other two set up each shot, enact a part when necessary, and cue the music. Fortunately, more often than not, at least one class member is skilled in handling the camera and can film all the poetry videos. If not, it is easy to train one or two students to film. Often students need to use their free time for the actual filming so that they can make multiple attempts until they are satisfied with the final product.

Once all the poems have been put on video, students view the results. Students love to see their own work and that of others. Many of the poetry videos turn out to be very clever, even professional. Some reveal a particular sensitivity to language and imagery. Students submit the actual video, the storyboard for the video, and a written explanation of their audiovisual presentation of the poem.

Poetry approached this way comes alive for all students, especially the disenchanted. By emulating a form they know, the music video, students gain new insight into the visual possibilities of the poetry and a new appreciation for poetry.

We want to take advantage of students' new interest in poetry to develop their ability to create their own poems. To give them something to work from, we show a short film that features a sport. Several good films are available, but *Descent* (Wombat Productions) works especially well. This 12-minute film has virtually no dialogue, only images and a music soundtrack. The film documents the preparation of a downhill skier for an international competition. The filmmaker follows the skier from the practice slopes to the starting gate, down the slope to what appears to be victory, only to end in defeat. The final sequence shows the skier back on the practice slopes preparing for another competition.

We show the film twice. The first time students simply enjoy watching it. The second time, we ask them to make a list of everything they see and hear. They tell us they can write down what they see, but because there is no dialogue they don't know what sounds to record. We tell them to listen for sounds of the skis on the snow, the sounds of the crowd, and the countdown of the gatekeeper. As they watch the film the second time, we write what we hear on the chalkboard to give them some ideas of what to listen for. We write down onomatopoetic words, such as *swoosh, swish, roar, groan, ooh, aah,* and *beep.* We also write down words describing what we see, such as *slip, slide, twist, turn, swoop, glide, thrust, crouch, lean, bend, jump, soar,* and *fall.* Armed with these words and the images of the story in our minds, we challenge the students to retell the story of the downhill skier in poetic form. We tell them they will create their own poetic form, one that reflects the action of the story. To give them an idea of how to create a form, we compose a poem based on the words we have recorded on the board. Ruth arranged her words to resemble the pattern of the skier's descent.

Descent

A swish
   breaks
      the silence
         of the frozen slope
           the skier skims
       the surface
    of the packed powder.
      Strong sinews overreach themselves.

He strives
   for speed
     competing
        against
          himself.

          Strong,
       sure of
     success
       he swoops
        down
          the slope
            sliding
          slipping
       succumbing
to the tyranny of silent snow.

We tell the students that this kind of poetry is called *shaped* or *concrete poetry*. We ask them what decisions Ruth made in writing this poem. For example, she had to decide on what part of the film to focus. Obviously she chose one segment in the skier's preparation for the race. We ask them what other decisions she had to make. They mention the layout of the words, the sequence of the words, and the words themselves. Students always notice the emphasis on sibilance, especially the initial s. We remind them that this repetition of initial consonants is called alliteration. Ruth tells them she chose such words for their onomatopoetic value; she wanted to try to recreate the actual sounds of the film in the sounds of the words.

Now the students are ready to try their hands at creating a shaped poem based on their notes from the film. We encourage them as they draft, suggesting onomatopoetic and alliterative words to help them tell their part of the story. We suggest that they imagine what the skier might be thinking and feeling at the moment in the story they choose to retell in their poem. We look at Ruth's poem again, pointing out words she chose to reveal his thoughts and feelings, such as "He strives for speed," and "strong, sure of success" and "succumbing to the tyranny of silent snow." We want them to convey their ideas of the skier's inner life in their poems. Once they are satisfied with their poems, we photocopy them to share with the class.

Before students lose interest in poetry, we make a dramatic shift. We ask students to write about their favorite sports, indicating what experiences they have had either as players or spectators. Students write about their love of tennis, commitment to track, their frustrations with lacrosse, and their successes with basketball. Eric wrote about his enthusiasm for cycling.

> Throughout my life I have always enjoyed bike riding. Ever since I first learned how to pedal down the driveway of my home, I knew that bike riding would be a part of my life forever. As a young boy I had a dirt bike, which still sits in our garage to this day, cob webs and all. Once I outgrew this little dirt bike, I did not get a new one right away. I figured I would be driving a car soon and did not think a new bike would be worth the investment. But one day as I walked home from school, I happened to stumble across a old ten-speed bike at a rummage sale. I bought it for a song, took it home, fixed it up, made sure everything was safe and in proper working condition; then I began to ride. As weeks turned into months, I rode more and more. I enjoyed the ability of having full control over my speed and destination. Gradually, as I was able to go faster and had enough endurance to keep that speed up, I began to feel unsafe using this old bike. I had ridden this bike to its maximum as far as peddling and speed were concerned; I felt I needed something a little safer, a bike that was made for high speed and long distances. I needed a bike that would enable me to push my body and my machine to their limits. I needed a racing bike. That summer I bought exactly what I needed.

As we share the journals, we make a list on the board of the various sports students enjoy. The list usually includes the standard basketball, football, and baseball, as well as lacrosse, tennis, track, swimming, cycling, horseback riding, bowling, wrestling, karate, gymnastics, hiking, skiing, surfing, soccer, and sailing. To take advantage of their interest in so many sports, we assign the reading of a biography of a sports luminary, preferably one involved in a sport of interest to the individual student. Our school and community librarians prepare bibliographies of available sports biographies. Students read the biographies on their own, keeping a reader-response journal about their books. In these journals they record what they learn about the athlete by asking themselves the same questions they ask in the initial activity in this unit: "What made him or her an outstanding athlete? What obstacles did he or she have to overcome? What contributions did she or he make to the game and to the world at large?" This time they have much more detail in response to these questions. In addition, students include personal responses to the athlete, such as what they most admire or dislike in the sports figure.

While they are reading, we introduce the idea of creating a sports magazine as a class activity. Again we divide students into groups, but this time groups of five. We structure them so that each one has a student with some artistic ability, one with computer expertise, and one with strong writing skills. We ask them to bring to class samples of the sports magazines they read. We bring in some too. These include *Sports Illustrated, Bicycling, Golf, Runner's World, Sail, Flying, Motor Cyclist, Outdoor Life, and Inside Sports.* Their groups examine the magazines and make a list of the kinds of articles typically included in them. They find articles describing particular games/events, athletes, coaches, training and fitness, success stories, and problems involved in sports, such as drugs, injuries, and corruption.

We tell students they are to write at least three articles each for their group magazine. Included in the magazine will be at least three "news" stories covering a game or competition, at least three feature stories about a student athlete or a coach, at least two editorials focusing on a problem, issue, or success, and at least two reviews of sports biographies. We encourage students to embellish their magazines with additional features, such as games, puzzles, anecdotes, jokes, and letters: to include poems they wrote earlier in the unit; and, where appropriate, to illustrate their articles with photographs and drawings. Students meet in groups to assign themselves the work.

To teach students how to write the type of article they have been assigned in their groups, we temporarily regroup students into feature-article groups, news story groups, and editorial groups. While we work with students in one group, the others use class time to read biographies.

We work with the news article group first so that students have time to cover school games while we are working with other groups. First we analyze some model articles from newspapers and magazines that cover individual games. We have used an article by Michael Martinez about the Rose Bowl game that appeared in *The New York Times* on January 1, 1991. We help students see that, as in other news articles, the lead paragraph in a sports article answers the five W questions: who, what, where, when, and why. However, unlike other news articles, which move from the most important to the least important details, the typical sports article summarizes the key moments in the game chronologically, highlighting major plays by specific players. In a sports article it is very important to give credit to the athletes who make particularly notable plays or score the game's winning points.

The model article ends with the last major touchdown of the game. Other sports articles may end with a summary statement about how well the team is doing to date as a result of their victory in this particular game. Because sports events take place after school and on weekends, we have to allow about a week for students to cover a game and gather the data to write their news articles. Prior to sending students out to cover a game, we have them meet briefly in their original groups to achieve group consensus on which games taking place that week are to be covered for inclusion in their magazine. Once this decision has been made, we encourage our news reporters to take copious notes during the game they are responsible for covering. The following week, when all of them have had ample time to attend a game and gather details, we meet with the news article group again. We help them select from their extensive notes about the game those facts that best recapture the event. Organization of details is not a major issue because most of the time they will simply recount the game as it occurred. However, our students need assistance in writing the lead paragraph and in deciding how to end their piece.

Seth wrote about a recent swim meet:

The Yorktown boys swim team gave a strong showing at the Gene Misture Invitational on Saturday, Feb. 5 at Mt. Vernon High School, clinching the second place trophy in a field of eight schools.

The Yorktown team, which totaled 272 points in the 12 events, was beaten only by the homefield Mt. Vernon team, which tallied 385 points.

Coach Mara Galassi was happy with her team's performance, saying, "I was really pleased. We fell exactly where I wanted us to fall. Many of the kids were trying new events for the first time."

YHS sophomore Jim Wall shone particularly brightly as the only non–Mt. Vernon participant to capture first place in two events. Jim won the 100 (meter) freestyle with a time of 0:55:31 and the 200 free-style with a time of 2:04.72 which was also a personal best for him.

Wall was happy with the team's showing. "Everyone swam great," he said. "Mt. Vernon was pretty tough. We lost to them in the regular season."

The team, which entered the meet with a 4-2 record, has two matches remaining in their regular season, Peekskill on Feb. 5 and Gorton on Feb. 7.

Ken covered a basketball game:

On Wednesday, the Varsity Basketball team stunned undefeated league leader John Jay 59–58 in overtime.

The game was exciting, as the Huskers held a 37–24 lead at half-time, only to watch the Indians storm back to tie the game 53–53 at the end of regulation time. Both the Huskers and the Indians had a chance to win the game, but Yorktown missed a shot with eight seconds remaining and John Jay missed at the buzzer.

In overtime, Yorktown went ahead 59–53, with several opportunities to seal the victory, however, missed free throws down the stretch hurt them. John Jay had the opportunity to tie the game at 55, but Greg Bradford swatted away a Steve Silas jump shot. Eventually the Indians, on the strength of a Silas three pointer, brought the Indians within one, 59–58. On the ensuing inbounds play, the Huskers' Alex Mojica was fouled, but missed the first free throw. John Jay grabbed the rebound and took the ball upcourt. However, they inexplicably called time out with one second remaining and did not have enough time to get off a game-winning shot.

The victory snapped John Jay's eight game league winning streak, and improved the Huskers record to 9–10 (4–6 in the league).

While members of the news article group are gathering their data by attending games and working on their biographies during class time, we meet with the feature-article group. We ask each group member to choose a sport to write about and to begin by interviewing other students in the school who are active participants in that sport. We encourage them to interview at least five student athletes. To prepare them for the interviews, we work together to develop questions they can ask that will elicit personal responses about the individual's interest in and commitment to that sport. Some of the questions students have asked include:

- How did you get involved in the sport?
- How much time do you devote to it?
- What do you like most about it?
- What was your most thrilling moment as a participant?
- Who has influenced you most in the sport?

We also ask them to interview several people who particularly enjoy watching the sport. Here, too, we brainstorm questions they can ask to get meaningful data about why people spend so much time watching that particular sport. Our students have asked such questions as:

- What interests you about the sport?
- What was your most thrilling moment as a spectator?
- Who are your favorite sports figures and teams?
- What do you enjoy most about watching the sport?

We send students throughout the school, especially to the cafeteria, the gym, the library, the student lounge, wherever students congregate. We also encourage them to talk to students between classes and after school.

When students return to class after having completed their interviews, they are eager to share their results with each other. We allow them time to talk about what they learned. Then we help them organize their interviews. We look at models of feature articles from sports sections of newspapers and in sports magazines to determine the pattern such articles typically follow. We want to show them how to develop an interesting, attention-getting lead. We also use the model to show them how to incorporate quotes from their sources into a general article, rather than follow a question-answer format. An excellent model is George Vecsey's column "Sports of the Times," published in *The New York Times* on March 31, 1991, in which he discusses concerns about soccer star Diego Armando Maradona, who is in trouble because of his cocaine use. The article begins with a year-old quotation from a leading soccer official predicting Diego Armando Maradona's fall, follows that with a general discussion of the popularity of soccer and boxing for people wanting to escape poverty, then details the meteoric rise to athletic success of Maradona, ending with his fall from grace because of an addiction that led to the squandering of his talent and finally to his exile from the sport.

Once students have read and analyzed the structure of this piece, we ask them to look at another piece. This time we choose one that shows a sports figure in a positive light, such as one from the series entitled a "Season of Dreams" by Sara Rimer in *The New York Times,* during the week of June 18–25, 1991. In this series Ms. Rimer traces the success of Washington High School's Dominican baseball stars' efforts to use their athletic prowess to improve their lives educationally and economically.

Having examined at least two pieces, our students are ready to look at their own material and shape it into logical sections. Following Vecsey's pattern, they begin with a quote from someone whom they have interviewed, and they continue with an analysis of the sport's appeal. Students usually go into considerable detail in the middle of their feature articles as they recount several memorable anecdotes that were shared with them. Many of our students have chosen to end their articles with personal references to their own interest in the sport.

Invariably students find being selective very difficult. They feel compelled to use all the data they gather. We help them see the need for making choices and including only the most vivid and interesting portions. Sometimes they find they need to talk to at least one of their respondents again to get enough specific details to retell the experience well. We allow time for them to do that. Other students decide that the material from one of their interviews is so interesting that they want to do the entire piece on one person. In this case, too, it is often necessary for them to conduct a follow-up interview to get additional data. Katie, who interviewed our highest-scoring lacrosse star, was intrigued by his comment that he had no intention of playing lacrosse in college but felt his high school experience had been important far beyond what it taught him about the sport. She interviewed him again to get more details about the benefits he had only alluded to in the earlier interview. He expanded on his belief that he had learned so much about cooperation, sharing, and sportsmanship that his participation in the lacrosse team had changed him as a person. As a result, Katie shaped her whole piece around this insight.

Brian was intrigued by the controversy about admitting Pete Rose to the Baseball Hall of Fame. At the same time, he had been reading a biography of Hank Aaron and was particularly impressed with his outstanding career in baseball. Brian decided to do his feature on Hank Aaron as the model of baseball greats against whom all candidates to the Hall of Fame should be measured. He wrote:

A misty rain fell in Atlanta, Georgia on the evening of April 8, 1974 in the Atlanta Braves Stadium. Hank Aaron waited patiently for Al Downing to throw him a pitch.

The Dodger lefty wound up and threw. "Ball one," the umpire shouted. Downing wound up again and threw his fastball. That was the pitch Hank had been waiting for. Crack! The ball soared over the infield, the outfield, and the left center field fence into the Braves bull pen.

Hank Aaron had just hit his 715th home run, breaking Babe Ruth's forty year old record of 714.

Hank Aaron's success has been well earned. When he was fourteen he chose four goals: play in the major leagues, win the batting championship, be the Most Valuable Player, and play in the World Series. In 1956, Hank won the batting title with a .328 average. His 200 hits and 34 doubles were the best in the National League! On September 23, 1957, Hank hit a home run in the bottom of the eleventh inning to clinch the pennant for the Braves. Hank finished the 1957 season leading the league in homers (44), hits (198), total bases (369) and RBI's (132). In 1958 he won a Gold Glove for being the league's best right fielder. In 1959, Hank won his second National League batting crown with a 355 average. He led the league in hits, total bases and home runs. 1963 was one of Aaron's best years. He led the league in home runs, RBI's, hits, and total bases. Because he played so well, he was voted the National League's "Player of the Year." For the thirteenth year in a row, he was voted to the All Star team. On May 17, 1970, Hank drove out his 3000th hit.

During his career he played in 3,298 games. He hit 3,771 hits for second on the all-time list. He led the league in home-runs (755) and RBI's (2297). His career batting average was .305 with 624 doubles, 98 triples, 240 stolen bases and he scored 2,174 runs. Hank Aaron's record proves he was one of the best baseball players ever.

In addition to his accomplishments as a baseball player, Hank Aaron is also a very special human being. He has always worked for worthwhile causes, especially those that try to find cures for children's diseases. He has also spoken out on behalf of civil rights for Blacks. He has been a model citizen. One team manager said, "I have never met a better man or a finer gentleman."

For his extraordinary record in baseball and for the kind of person he is, I believe that Hank Aaron should be recognized as the ideal athlete and the model against which all other players are judged for acceptance into the Baseball Hall of Fame.

Once we have helped the feature-article writers organize their pieces, we do the same for the editorial writers. Because all students are writing three articles, they may be working in two or more groups at once. Most of the students in this last group will be working on their second article at this point. Again we go to models to determine what sports-related issues merit editorial comment in the magazines. Our students find articles commenting on equality of opportunity for women, residual racism in sports, abuse of drugs, corruption scandals, brutality in boxing, academic eligibility for athletes, controversial players and managers, poor sportsmanship, and violence in the stands.

As our students begin to draft their editorials, we remind them of what they know about persuasive essay writing, reviewing the idea that they should take a position on an issue and develop several reasons to support it. A helpful model is the article by Larry Merchant on boxing published in the sports section of *The New York Times*, March 3, 1991, which Mr. Merchant analyzes the issue of when a fight should be stopped, arguing against the old idea that only the final bell or a decisive knockout should stop a fight. He suggests that a fight should be stopped when a fighter is being punished and when he has no hope of winning because he is too far behind. To prove his case, he illustrates with a number of tragedies that have occurred in boxing that could have been prevented by a timely ending of the matches. We review the structure of this model to help students see how to support their position in the editorials they are writing.

Once students select a topic, they decide on the position they wish to take and then determine at least two reasons to support that position. When their purposes are clear, they begin to gather information by talking to coaches and administrators and by reading articles on their subjects in the library. When they return to class, we help them organize their data and support their position with specific data, encouraging them to use the informal, anecdotal style characteristic of most sports writers. Allison found the major issue worthy of editorial comment in Yorktown High School to be that of academic standards for student athletes. She wrote:

> At a recent faculty meeting, several teachers at our school criticized the absence of any academic requirements for student participation in athletics. They cited statistics of football and lacrosse players who were failing their courses and yet were allowed to play in varsity competition. As a result, they wish to impose an academic requirement on all student athletes. I believe that imposing any academic requirements for participation in sports is ridiculous.
>
> For some students, sports is the only thing that keeps them from dropping out of school. According to our athletic director, at least four of last year's seniors would not have graduated except for their involvement in the championship lacrosse team. One player told me he hates school but comes every day because of practice. "Once I am here," he says, "I might as well go to class." If this student was dropped from the team because he didn't meet some arbitrary academic standard, he wouldn't even bother to come to school much less go to class.
>
> Beside, sports participation actually helps students perform better in their academic classes. They learn discipline through the long, hard hours of practice necessary to master their sport. This discipline has to help students in their academic life as well. Moreover, coaches have a lot of influence on their student athletes. We know of several coaches who encourage their players not only to go to class but to keep up with the work. Coach Turnbull says, "My best athletes compete in the classroom too. I tell them I want to be proud of them both on and off the field." This kind of influence is far better than the threat of having to meet an academic requirement for participation in sports.

Once students have drafted their news stories, features, and editorials, they reassemble in their original magazine groups to get assistance in editing and revising their work from other members of the group. Because they have been reading the biographies of sports stars during this entire project, we ask them to include promotional material selling their biographies as advertisements in their magazines. Each ad should cover a full page and capture the flavor of the sports star's life and contributions. Students then work together on the additional articles, illustrations, and special features that will make their magazine unique. They need at least four class periods at this stage to go over their material, type it, decide on the sequence of the articles, design a cover, and put the magazine together.

We put completed magazines in the library, invite the principal to an awards presentation for the best magazine with ribbon awards for each category: best news story, feature, book review, editorial, artwork and layout, fillers, and best overall magazine. We ask the school newspaper to cover the awards ceremony and publish photographs of winning students as well as include an article about their achievements.

Sports participation may not result in professional careers for any of our disenchanted students, but their love of sports can certainly lead to success in the English class. To celebrate that success, we end "A Sporting Life" by showing a full-length film, such as *Field of Dreams* or *The Natural.*

Bibliographies

Films

Chase the Wind Sports Films Library. Land speed racing.
Descent (Wombat Productions). Skiing.
The Fighter (Wombat Productions). Boxing.
Jackie Robinson Story (Hearst Screen News Digest). Baseball.
Mood of Surfing (PPP Films).
Rosey Grier: The Courage to Be (Churchill Films). Football.

Books: Sports Biographies

Biracree, Tom. *Althea Gibson.* New York: Chelsea House 1989.
Blue, Vida. *Vida: His Own Story.* New Jersey: Prentice Hall, 1972.
Dolan, Edward F. *Archie Griffin.* New York: Doubleday, 1977.
Dolan, Edward F. *Janet Guthrie: First Woman Driver at Indianapolis.* New York: Doubleday, 1978.
Dowet, Don. *Vida: Doming Up Again.* New York: GP Putnam & Sones, 1974.
Foyt, A. J. *A. J.* New York: Warner Books, 1983.
Gallagher, Mark. *Explosion! (Mickey Mantle).* New York: Arbor House, 1987.
Green, Bill. *Jack Dempsey.* New York: Sam Har Press, 1974.
Goolagong, Evonne. *Evonne: On the Move.* New York: Dutton, 1975.
Gutman, Bill. *Jim Plunkett.* New York: Grosset & Dunlap, 1973.
Gutman, Bill. *Hank Aaron.* New York: Grosset & Dunlap, 1973.
Hahn, James. *Henry: The Sporting areer of Henry Aaron* New Yok: Crestwod House, 1982.
Hahn, James. *Walt: The Sports Career of Wilton Chamberlain.* New York: Crestwood House, 1981.

Hamil, Dorothy, with Elva Clairmont. *Dorothy Hamill on and off the Ice.* New York: Alfred A. Knopf, 1983.

Haney, Lynn. *Chris Evert, The Young Champion.* New York: Putnam, 1976.

Heidenreich, Steve. *Running Back.* New York: Hawthhorne Books, 1979.

Johnson, Davey. *Bats.* New York: GP Putnam & Sones, 1986.

Kramer, Jerry. *Instant Replay: The Green Bay.* New York: American Library, 1968.

Mantle, Mickey. *The Mick.* New York: Jove Books, 1985.

Mays, Willie. *Say Hey.* New York: Pocket Books, 1988.

McCarver, Tim. *Oh Baby, I Love It!* New York: Villard Books, 1987.

McMahon, Jim. *McMahon!* New York: Warner Books, 1987.

Nascimento, Edson. *My Life and the Beautiful Game: The Autobiography of Pele.* New York: Doubleday, 1977.

Navratilova, Martina, with George Vecsey. *Martina.* New York: Fawcett Crest, 1985.

Ott, Melvin T. *Mel Ott Story.* New York: Juliam Messner, 1939.

Pinella, Lou. *Sweet Lou.* New York: GP Putnam & Sones, 1986.

Prugh, Jeff. *Herschel Walker.* New York: Random House, 1983.

Rosenthal, Bert. *Darryl Dawkins, The Master of Disaster.* Chicago: Children's Press, 1982.

Schoor, Gene. *Bob Turley, Fireball Pitcher.* New York: GP Putnam & Sons, 1959.

Scott, Richard. *Jackie Robinson.* New York: Chelsea House, 1987.

Stambler, Irwin. *Catfish Hunter: The Three Million Dollar Arm.* New York: GP Putnam & Sons, 1976.

Stingley, Darryl. *Darryl Stingley: Happy to Be Alive.* New York: Beaufort Books, 1983.

Williams, Ted. *My Turn at Bat.* New York: Pocket Books, 1971.

Addendum
Storyboard Instuctions for Poetry Videos:
Definition of Terms*

ECU:Extreme Close-up. This shot would contain only facial detail, usually from the top of the eyes to the bottom of the mouth.

CU:Close-up. This shot frequently is used in news programs. It starts at the top of the head and ends at the top of the shoulders.

MCU:Medium Close-up. This shot commonly is used in interviews and some news broadcasts. It is often called a bust shot. This shot begins at the top of the head and ends at the bust.

---

*Adapted from a student-written instructions manual for the creation of a storyboard.

<u>MWS:Medium Wide Shot</u>. This shot is often used in fitness programs, where shots of an entire person's body are needed.

<u>WS:Wide Shot</u>. This shot often is used on sports coverage when a large playing area must be shown.

<u>TWS:Extreme Wide Shot</u>. This shot is performed by zooming the camera lens all the way out until it can capture as much as possible. It is used at football games when the director wants the camera to shoot as much as possible of the field.

HELP WANTED

Two roads diverged in a yellow wood,
And sorry I could not travel both
And be one traveler, long I stood
And looked down one as far as I could
To where it bent in the undergrowth;

Then took the other, as just as fair,
And having perhaps the better claim,
Because it was grassy and wanted wear;
Though as for that the passing there
Had worn them really about the same,

And both that morning equally lay
In leaves no step had trodden black.
Oh, I kept the first for another day!
Yet knowing how way leads on to way,
I doubted if I should ever come back.

I shall be telling this with a sigh
Somewhere ages and ages hence:
Two roads diverged in a wood, and I—
I took the one less traveled by,
And that has made all the difference.
            "The Road Not Taken" by Robert Frost

One of the greatest problems in engaging disenchanted students is overcoming their sense that what goes on in the classroom has little or no relevance to their real lives. No matter how interesting we believe our lessons are, students often find them unrelated to the world they inhabit. This chapter addresses this concern by focusing on real-life skills: writing application letters and résumés, interviewing strategies, coping with on-the-job problems, and researching career options. What could be more relevant to teenagers than helping them choose a career "road" to follow?

We begin by having students consider what constitutes their ideal job and to record their ideas in journals. Then we ask them to share their thinking so that we can get a sense of the kinds of issues we need to explore to help them discover their "roads." What Chris wrote is representative of their responses:

> I really don't know what I want to do with my life. Even thinking about making a decision like that is scary. I do know though that I don't want to sit behind a desk all day. I get restless and need a job where I am free to move around. I think I would like to travel as part of my job. I love seeing new places and meeting new people. I need a job that isn't routine too, one where I get to do many different things as part of my work day. Of course, I also want to make a lot of money and have people look up to me because of what I do. I'd like to make a difference in people's lives if I can. I like to help people.

As students read their entries, we list on the board or the overhead projector the characteristics they mention most often when describing their future careers. They all want positions that offer variety, interest, respect, purpose, and money. We then talk about how to explore career possibilities and work on skills they will need for any career. To help each of them discover potential careers, we develop an interest inventory that includes categories to determine favorite courses, interests, competencies, values, goals, favored locations, and desired working environment. (See the Addendum at the end of this chapter.)

Students enjoy filling out these interest inventories. However, the material in them is personal enough that they prefer sharing them in small groups rather than reading them aloud to the entire class. Then we ask students to list possible careers for one another, as many as they can at this point, careers that they think would capitalize on their interests and strengths. We model this process by sharing with them our completed interest inventories and then listing our career options. Naturally, teaching is one of those options, for us, one that correlates with many of our interests and strengths.

Of course we acknowledge that identifying possible career goals is not the same as achieving them. For that we all need to learn some strategies for success. To get started we show the film *Climb*, in which two young men prepare carefully for their ascent of El *Capitan* in Yosemite. The film can be viewed as a parable of modern life, depicting a person's struggle for success: self-confidence coupled with recognition of one's dependence on others. Students watch the film twice. After the first viewing they write for a few moments in their journals about their overall impressions of the climb and relate the experience to their own lives. Anthony wrote:

> I've always wanted to do something really scary like that. I mean, they risked their lives to get to the top. I was impressed by how carefully they got ready for their climb. They didn't leave anything to chance. I was surprised by how hard they had to work, just planning out each move up the rock face. And they really had to concentrate and trust themselves and each other. I don't know whether I'd want my life to depend on someone else so much, though. What a great feeling they had at the end there. They acted as though they had conquered the world. The closest I ever came to an experience like that was on a camping trip last summer. Me and my buddy were totally on our own for the first time in our lives. We only had what we could carry on our backs, including our sleeping bags. Our lives

were not in danger, but it was kind of scary and fun too, especially at night. At the end of the weekend, we were tired and dirty and full of bites, but we felt really good about ourselves because we had hiked a whole 25 miles.

We show the film a second time and ask the students to take careful notes on the stages the climbers go through and the qualities they exhibit at each stage. We model the process for the first few minutes of the film, making sure we include direct quotes. In our discussion afterwards we focus on the quotes and identify the qualities reflected in them. For example, one of the climbers says, "You have to make a physical and mental commitment to climb. You have to prepare for it; you can't do it until you're ready." Later he says, "When you're out there, you find out what you're all about. You drive yourself beyond your limits." The other climber says, "You've got to commit to it, to stand on that pin. Finally you just have to trust yourself." We talk about how important commitment, self-reliance, and trust are in enabling the climbers to reach their goal: the top of El Capitan.

Now they go back to their interest inventories and examine the goals they stated there. We want them to identify the personal qualities they can tap in pursuit of their goals. More often than not, however, they tend to describe situations in which they have achieved a goal. They need our help to determine the qualities reflected in these situations. Invariably our students, without realizing it, reveal qualities such as persistence, enthusiasm, optimism, courage, and insight. Because disenchanted students frequently lack a positive self-image, they are surprised and pleased when we point out the many positive qualities they have revealed. We ask them to consider what essential quality they think they need to succeed, one the rock climbers clearly manifest, but one they have yet to develop. Predictably, students identify self-confidence. They recognize that they lack faith in their own abilities; they do not trust themselves. Together we set as their goal improving their sense of self-worth. We ask them, "What would make you feel good about yourselves?" After the initial responses about getting an A in our course, being the most popular guy or girl in school, or winning the lottery, students admit that getting a meaningful job and earning a good income would give them the self-confidence they lack.

Again we refer to the climbers in the film, identifying the steps in their preparation to achieve their goal of reaching the top of the mountain. From here it is easy to make the transition from the climbers' preparation to that necessary for our students to succeed in finding good jobs.
We list the steps:

- Reading help-wanted ads.
- Writing a résumé.
- Writing a cover letter.
- Making follow-up telephone calls.
- Having an interview.
- Writing a follow-up letter.

To give them an opportunity to acquire these skills, we ask students to pretend they are in the process of looking for a job—as, in fact, many of them are.

To prepare them for their job search, we teach them how to write a résumé. Those students who attend technical classes or take business courses and already have résumés bring them in to share as models. Because students learn best from each other, we use these students, whenever possible, as instructors to help the others develop helpful, informative résumés. We stress that brevity is critical in a résumé because employers are often inundated with responses to their ads and won't even look at those that are too long, messy, or poorly prepared. We instruct students to compress all the relevant data about themselves onto one sheet of white paper and to be sure to type the résumé. Near the top of the left side they type their names and full address. On the right side they supply their phone number. They then put their data into categories:

- Position desired.
- Educational background (last school first, including the years attended, probable date of graduation and course of study).
- Employment experience (most recent experience first, years or months at that position, and job responsibilities).
- Volunteer experience.
- Honors and achievements.
- Personal data (gender, marital status, health).
- References.

Our students do not necessarily have to include every category in their résumés. For example, if they have earned no honors or achievements, they may delete that category. At the same time, we caution them always to tell the truth, never to fictionalize or exaggerate their qualifications. We also advise them to request permission before including anyone's name as a reference.

Students work on their résumés in the computer lab. We circulate around the room, assisting them in finding the most attractive format for the data they wish to present. Because they know these résumés can actually be used, they are concerned enough about correctness to make use of the computer's spell check and to ask for peer help in editing their final products. Diana worked hard on her résumé to present herself in the most favorable light—see page following.

Once students have completed their résumés, they have a better idea of their marketable strengths. Now they are ready to review help-wanted ads and select a position for which to apply. We give them a sheet of ads created from help-wanted columns in local newspapers. To help them interpret these ads, we review some of the abbreviations they may find, such as PT (part-time), FT (full-time), temp (temporary), exp (experience[d]), bg (background), asst (assistant), and ns (nonsmoking).

Diana M. Calamita   (914) 555-6060
2760 Sunnyside Avenue
Yorktown Heights, New York 10598

POSITION DESIRED

Word processing

EDUCATION

Yorktown High School, 1987-1991
Technical Center Information Systems, 1989-1991

WORK EXPERIENCE

Yorktown High School, Yorktown Heights
Social Studies Department
October 1990-June 1991
Typist

International Business Machines Corporation, Yorktown Heights, October
1990 - Present
Assistant Secretary

VOLUNTEER EXPERIENCE

School newspaper

ACHIEVEMENTS

Yorktown High School Track Award, 1990-1991
Technical Center Awards in Skills Olympics, 1989-1991

PERSONAL DATA

Female, single, excellent health

REFERENCES

Gordon Baptiste, Social Studies Instructor, Yorktown High School, 2727
Crompond Rd., Yorktown, NY 10598

Judy DiLucchio, International Business Machines, Rte. 134, Yorktown
Heights, NY 10598

Sample ads:

■ Activities assistant: to complement dynamic team, work steady Sundays 9am-4:30pm. Additional time possible. Seek reliable, creative person who enjoys giving to the elderly. Box PN14.

After-school games assistant: High school student needed to run various games and activities in after-care program for grades K-2. 3pm-4:30pm. on Wednesday and/or Thursday. Seek reliable, caring, athletically skilled individual. Respond Box PN18.

Baby sitter needed: for 5-year-1 & 19-month-old boys. Regular basis every Saturday night, plus occasional weeknight. Seek loving, responsible, non-smoking applicant. Own transportation. High school OK. Respond Box PN34.

Certified lifeguard: for summer camp program, hours 9-4. Children ages 3-10. Respond Box PN A97.

Chef's assistant: Banquet affairs, Thurs to Sunday. Club facility. Salary based on experience. Respond Box PN36.

Groundskeeper: Summer. Exp. landscaping bg. Health care facility. Light maintenance duties. Responsible, clean, driver's license. Respond Box PN B23.

Hair salon: needs PT shampoo assistant weekends, exp. a must. Respond James Carroll, Box PN09.

Library clerk: 15 hours/wk 6pm-9pm. Good pay. Experienced, responsible. High school student OK. Box PN32.

Stock clerk afternoons and Saturdays: excellent opportunity for bright, ambitious young person. Box PN07.

Students select one ad to which they respond in a letter. In it they cite the skills and other qualities they have that will enable them to do the best possible job, and they mention any relevant experience. They address their letters to the appropriate box number in their city and state.

Before they begin drafting their letters, we review business letter format, instructing them to be simple and direct, to indicate their qualifications for the position advertised, and to request an interview.

Before students write their letters, we give them two sample letters and ask for their reactions. One letter is full of errors and adopts an arrogant tone. The other is a respectful and well-presented introduction of the individual. We discuss their impressions of the two letters, asking which one is likely to gain a favorable response.

98 Hyatt Drive
Pleasantville, CA 92100
May 15, 1991

Camp Director
Box PN A97
Pleasantville, CA 92100

Dear Camp Director:

I am replying to your advertisement for a certified lifeguard in the May 14 issue of the <u>Pleasantville Gazette.</u> I would like to be considered for that position.

I am an experienced lifeguard and have worked at the local community center pool for the past three summers. I love working with little children and am especially good at helping them overcome their fear of putting their heads in water. Last fall, I gave swimming lessons to a group of 6- and 7-year-olds.

I would appreciate the opportunity to discuss my qualifications with you. I can be reached at 555-8409 after 4 p.m.

Thank you for your consideration.

Sincerely,

Jerry Jones

Jerry Jones

Dear PNA97,

I saw your ad and I want you to know I'm the man for you. I'm a great life-gard, I know everything about it and I know how to keep kids in line. And I have a lot of experence at the town pool and all the little kids really are crazy about me.

Sincerely
Jerry

PS: My phone number is 555-8409.

The discussion of the two letters is lively. Our students notice the errors in the first letter immediately and are amused by the inappropriate tone of the writer. They also comment particularly on the obvious care the second writer took to present the most favorable picture of himself to the camp director. The correct business letter form, the relevance of the information provided, the appropriate diction, and the mechanical correctness enhance the chances of the second letter writer getting the job.

With these models in mind, we give class time in the computer lab for students to write their application letters. Once students are satisfied with the form and content of their letters, we encourage them to make use of the spell-check provision of the word processing software. When they return to class, they select a proofreading partner to review their letter for accuracy and completeness. Because we have discussed model letters, students realize the relevance of this exercise and take their work seriously. They realize the importance of the letter's appearance and correctness in making a good first impression on a prospective employer.

We respond to each letter by scheduling practice interviews to which students are instructed to bring their résumés. In preparation, we begin by telling students what questions the interviewer is likely to ask them, such as:

- Why do you want to work for us?
- What qualifications do you have for this position?
- What courses are you best at in school?
- What are your career goals?
- What do you know about our company/organization?
- What are your hobbies and outside interests?
- If I were to call one of your references, what would he/she say about you?

Students then add any questions they may have been asked on interviews, such as:

- What kinds of grades do you get in school?
- Have you ever been in trouble with the police?

- Do you have transportation to work?
- Do you drink?

We urge them to be prepared with some questions to ask the employer as a strategy to reveal their interest in the position. They may ask about specific duties, working hours, working conditions, and salary, if these items have not already been discussed.

In pairs, students practice interviewing each other as preparation for the real thing. We invite the career counselor to interview students for the specific positions for which they are applying. When the career counselor is unavailable, we invite a representative from a local business college or one of our school's business teachers to conduct the interviews. Having someone from outside the class adds to the reality and seriousness of the interviews.

On the days of the interviews students must present the interviewer with their application letter and copy of their résumé. We also insist that they dress appropriately for the job for which they are applying: jackets and ties for the boys, skirts or dresses for the girls if they are applying for an office or sales job or any other position where they have to dress more formally. They may wear casual clothes—clean and neat, of course—for a job such as camp counselor or ground's keeper. But they should wear shoes, not sneakers, get rid of their chewing gum, and be well groomed and <u>on time</u>.

On days of the interviews, we arrange to videotape the students so they can assess their own performances. Each interview lasts about 10 minutes, which we realize is much shorter than most actual interviews will be. But our purpose is to give students a sample of the interview experience and an opportunity to learn how to handle themselves in what can sometimes be a stressful situation, especially for students lacking self-confidence. Even though the interview practice is time consuming—it can take up to a week of class time to complete—class attention is focused on each student's performance. The videotaping adds a sense of importance to the proceedings. Students recognize the need to be a respectful audience so as not to interfere with the videotaped interview. Class members must pay close attention to every interview because they complete critique sheets for each other.

Name of applicant: _____

Position applied for: _____

Reason for acceptance or rejection: _____
_____

What the applicant did well:

Suggestions for improvement:

Name of reviewer: _____

We encourage students to comment on what they find commendable in each interview and to make specific suggestions for improvement.

We model the critique process by asking one student to take the role of the job applicant whom we interview for a position. At the end of the interview we guide the class in completing the critique sheet. On an overhead projection, we show how we would complete the form, emphasizing what the applicant did well, always being specific with any compliments or suggestions for improvement. Modeling our responses stimulates students to add their own specific observations. We review the critique sheets, noting the care with which each student has responded to the job applicant. Then we compile the critiques, to which we add our own, and give them to the job applicant. We take every opportunity to give positive feedback on our critique sheets, careful to remember that part of our goal is to help students improve their self-confidence. In most cases students who have carefully prepared for the interview by writing interesting and correct application letters, preparing accurate and complete résumés, asking intelligent questions, and conducting themselves appropriately at the interview are "hired."

Because we know that getting a job is one thing and holding onto it is another, we explore with our students the skills necessary for on-the-job success. Our career counselor is very helpful with this. Often we invite her to talk to our students about how they should dress and behave in certain difficult situations they may encounter with their employers or with the public in their new jobs. For example, some of our students who are chronically late for or absent from class are stunned to learn that their pay is docked for any time they miss on the job. To reinforce the importance of conscientious work habits, especially in a tight job market, we invite a number of employers from the local community who regularly hire teenagers to form a panel to discuss their experiences with teenage employees. They often mention the enthusiasm teenagers bring to the workplace, but they add that once the novelty has worn off, problems may follow. These can be avoided if teenage workers

- Get to work on time.
- Pay careful attention to their work
- Are courteous to the public.
- Work conscientiously.
- Dress and behave appropriately.
- Do not visit with their friends.
- Do not make personal phone calls.

We and the career counselor have already told the students many of the same things, but hearing all this from local employers adds validity to our words and to the unit. Students see that what we have been doing in class will help them be more marketable in a highly competitive job market.

The expectations identified by the employers seem to be reasonable and easy to accommodate. However, we recognize that when our students are actually on the job, they may have some trouble fulfilling these expectations and even more trouble handling the resulting problems. To facilitate their ability to cope, we divide students into groups to create scenarios dramatizing several difficult on-the-job situations. For example, one group enacts a scene in which a friend comes by to visit a teenage checker at a grocery store, distracting him from his duties.

Another group creates a dramatization of an irate customer venting her wrath on a teenage employee. Yet another group tackles the problem of the angry boss dissatisfied with the employee's performance. And, of course, one group must deal with the teenager coming to work late. Because students may have to cope with many other job-related difficulties, the scenarios vary from class to class. The point of the role-playing exercises remains the same: to empower our students with strategies for managing themselves successfully in the workplace.

Our attention thus far has been directed to helping students successfully implement their short-range job goals. But we have not forgotten the career goals they identified on the interest inventories. We now want our students to think beyond their after-school and summer employment to explore real career possibilities and determine what future training they may need.

To afford students an opportunity to explore a wide variety of careers, we plan a career fair for which each student becomes an expert on a career that is of interest to him or her. To initiate their research, students list in their journals several careers that interest them and two or three questions they have about each. Then they select careers to research. As a class we brainstorm the kinds of information they need, such as

- Educational requirements.
- Amount and type of training necessary.
- Job opportunities.
- Salary potential.
- General working conditions.

As a vital part of the research, they.interview someone engaged in that career to learn what it is actually like to work in that field, and, if possible, they "shadow" that person for at least a day. Most people, if they have been willing to be interviewed, are also willing to have a student join them for a day, going where they go, watching what they do, listening to what they say, and in general, getting a real feel for a day in the life of that career professional.

This research assignment provides students with opportunities to analyze, synthesize, and summarize three basic skills of critical literacy. And even more than in preceding activities, students take responsibility for their own learning. They select a topic of interest to them and determine how best to research it. They gain facility with such research skills as finding the best sources of information, gathering data, deciding what information to include, interviewing experts, organizing their material in a logical and engaging manner, and citing sources.

Because most people, especially the disenchanted, work best when they collaborate with others, we have students work with partners on this project. Partners can be assigned randomly; one method we like is to have half the class select from a hat pictures of people engaged in various careers. The other half of the class selects pictures of tools or other objects related to each career. Partnerships are formed as students match related pictures, such as a doctor and a stethoscope, a butcher and a cleaver, a fireman and a hose, and a hairdresser and a comb. Partners need not research the same topic, but they help each other through the research process. Each student keeps a double-entry log, recording on the left side the information she or he finds in the library, in the career center, and in interviews with people already engaged in that career. As information is collected and recorded, the partner reads the log and comments on the right side, responding to the information gathered, advising the writer about what still needs to be learned, and commenting on the progress of the research. In this way students help each other and assume more responsibility for their own learning. The log becomes one part of the information we use to assign grades to students at the end of the project. We grade the log based on our assessment of the student's serious study of sources of information available and the completeness of the record kept of that information.

Fred did his research on carpentry as a career. His log included information on different kinds of power saws used by carpenters:

> Most of these power saws are used for cutting wood for a straight cut or a miter cut like a 45 degree miter cut. The circular hand saw is one of the most common power tools used in carpentry. Carpenters use this saw right on the site where the project is located. This kind of saw can make all kinds of cuts. It can make compound cuts, which means you can make a 45 degree cut. The table saw is usually used inside where it will not get wet. It is a very good saw for indoor use. The radial arm saw is hooked up to a table or a bench. This saw is also good for making 45 degree cuts. There is another kind of saw called the "sawzall." This saw is usually used for putting up a wall partition where the top plate has to be shortened. It makes it easy for you to cut the piece off because of its long blade.
>
> Another kind of machine used in carpentry is the sander. There are many kinds of sanders, but for now I'll describe the belt sander and the rotating sander. There is also regular sandpaper, which is usually used for just touching up finished work. The belt sander is usually used for a large area like a table or something big. The rotating sander is usually used for something small. On both of these sanders you can put any grade sandpaper on it, meaning you can put different degrees of coarseness of paper on it.
>
> Squares are used for making a straight edge or a mitered edge. The framing square is used for any kind of work, usually work such as rafter layout or just simple edges. The T square comes in all different sizes, such as four feet or eight feet, also other sizes. This is used for framing out a four by eight piece of sheetrock. There is also a square called the speed square, which is used for straight angles or a 45 degree miter layout.

Once the research is completed, students are regrouped so that all those who researched the same career (or related careers) decide together how best to present their information at the career fair. For example, all students interested in the building trades (plumbers, carpenters, electricians, etc.) are together;

students interested in health-related fields (doctors, nurses, laboratory technicians, psychiatrists) are together; and so on. Each group is responsible for creating an informational flyer about its careers, for decorating a booth or a table appropriately, and for a poster and a sign. We photocopy sufficient numbers of the flyers so that those who attend the fair can take one if they wish. To increase interest and motivation, we invite other classes to attend the career fair. Our students act as experts and advise others on the advantages and opportunities of their careers. Members of the visiting classes may write letters to the "experts" requesting more information or commenting on what they learned about the careers at the fair.

To evaluate our students' performances, we assign a grade to each group based on our assessment of the career fair presentation and an individual grade based on each student's log and contributions to the group effort.

"Help Wanted" is designed to focus students on real-life topics: the skills necessary for finding and keeping jobs in the workplace and for making informed career choices that can make "all the difference" in their lives.

Addendum

Interest Inventory

Check off those items in each category that describe you

I am good at

_____ doing things with my hands
_____ eye-hand coordination
_____ athletics
_____ doing research
_____ talking with people
_____ imagining and visualizing
_____ problem solving
_____ working with people
_____ performing and entertaining
_____ negotiating and advising
_____ managing and leading others
_____ instructing
_____ other

I like to work with

_____ printed materials
_____ videos and audios
_____ computers
_____ machinery
_____ designs and symbols
_____ other

The "things" that interest me are

_____ machinery and tools
_____ building materials
_____ plants and trees
_____ animals
_____ household furnishings
_____ foods
_____ clothing
_____ electronic equipment
_____ games
_____ office equipment
_____ communications equipment
_____ forms of transportation
_____ equipment/instruments
_____ sports equipment
_____ music instruments
_____ artist's materials
_____ books
_____ other

My favorite subjects in school are

_____ English
_____ foreign language
_____ social studies/history
_____ science
_____ mathematics
_____ computer science
_____ business
_____ psychology
_____ health
_____ art
_____ music
_____ shop
_____ home economics
_____ physical education
_____ other

The kinds of people I like to work with are

_____ men
_____ women
_____ children
_____ adolescents
_____ mature people
_____ the elderly
_____ individuals

_____ groups
_____ all kinds of people

I like to work

_____ by myself
_____ with others
_____ as part of a team
_____ as a leader
_____ as one who carries out directions

Places I like to work are

_____ outside
_____ indoors
_____ in a large corporation
_____ in a small company
_____ at home
_____ at a desk
_____ in an office
_____ other

My ideal career would give me

_____ an opportunity to help others
_____ independence
_____ wealth
_____ power
_____ fame
_____ security
_____ influence
_____ excitement
_____ respect
_____ an opportunity to serve God
_____ an opportunity to be creative
_____ intellectual stimulation
_____ an opportunity to be a leader
_____ other

Resources for Career Research

These resources are available at most public libraries and school libraries or career centers. Many public libraries are also job information centers, which are serviced by career planners and librarians especially knowledgeable about sources of career information. In addition, most public libraries have a career file that includes pamphlets and other materials on jobs, training, education, and special recommendations for teenagers and the handicapped.

Books

Bolles, Richard Nelson. *What Color Is Your Parachute?* (Berkely, California, Ten Speed Press, 1990).

Bostwick, Burdette E. *Résumé Writing: A Comprehensive How to Do It Guide*, 3d ed. (New York, John Wiley, 1985).

Career Information Center, 3d ed. (Mission Hills, CA: Glencoe/Macmillan, 1987). Careers are defined and described, including requirements, employment outlook, opportunities for employment and advancement.

Eyler, David R. *Résumés That Mean Business.* (New York, Random House, 1990). Covers various kinds of résumés and cover letters, along with interviewing and the hiring process.

Figler, Howard. *The Complete Job-Search Handbook.* (New York: Holt, 1988).

Fowler, Elizabeth. *New York Times Career Planner.* (New York: Times Books, 1987). Describes various kinds of professional and vocational careers. Also contains helpful career planning information: education, education, assessing career trends, writing résumés, and on-the-job performance, including "The First Day."

Guide for Occupational Exploration, 2d ed. (Circle Pines, MN: AGS, 1984).

Hopke, William E., Ed. *Encyclopedia of Careers*, 8th ed. 4 vols. (Chicago: Ferguson Publishing Co., 1990). This encyclopedia has four volumes, titled *Industry Profiles, Professional Careers, General and Special Careers, and Technician's Careers.* Each volume covers, for each career, definitions, history, nature of work, requirements, opportunities for experience and exploration, methods of entering the field, advancement and employment outlook, average earnings, conditions of work, social and psychological factors, and related occupations.

Krannik, Ronald, and Caryl Krannik. *The Complete Guide to Public Employment.* (Woodbridge, VA: Impact Publication, 1986).

Prem, E. Russell, III, Ed. *Career Description Encyclopedia.* 6 vols. (Chicago: Ferguson Publishing Co., 1990).

U.S. Department of Labor. *Occupational Outlook Handbook.* (Washington, DC: U.S. Department of Labor, 1990; available from regional offices). Covers the nature of work, working conditions, employment, training, other qualifications, advancement, job outlook, earnings, related occupations, and sources of additional information.

Yate, Martin John. *Résumés That Knock 'em Dead.* (Holbrook, MA: Bob Adams, Inc., 1988).

Films

Career Planning (Journal Films). 16 min. Discusses setting career goals and fulfilling dreams.

Doing Your Eight (Journal Films). 20 min. Guidelines for getting and keeping a job.

The Interview Film (Barr Films). 21 min. What happens when five youth apply for the same job in a restaurant chain.

Job Hunt (Aims Instructional Media Service). 15 min. Step-by-step guide for getting a job.

Job Interview: Three Young Men (Churchill Films). 16 min. A hidden camera records three job interviews. The viewers are asked to judge which applicant(s) they would hire and why.

Job Interview: Three Young Women (Churchill Films). 16 min. The same format as the film above.

Your Job: Good Work Habits (Coronet Instructional Films). 13 min. High school students on their first full-time jobs discuss the importance of concentration, safety, friendliness, accuracy, and job satisfaction.

SHOW ME A STORY

"Once upon a time and a very good time it was there was a moocow coming down along the road and this moocow that was coming down along the road met a nicens little boy named baby tuckoo. . ."
His father told him that story.

Stephen Dedalus *from* Portrait of the Artist
as a Young Man, *by James Joyce*

"Tell us a story," children plead. "Tell us about the time you got lost"—or saved your brother from drowning, or flew in a plane all by yourself, or whatever events make up the fabric of our personal histories. These narratives capture our imaginations at any age by extending our experiences and allowing us to see life through the eyes of others. The earliest memory of James Joyce's hero, Stephen Dedalus, is of a "moocow" coming down a road, not a daily experience in young Stephen's life in Dublin, but vivid in his imagination because "his father told him that story" and made it come alive in his mind's eye.

We also want stories to come alive for our students, their imaginations to be engaged, and for them to become active readers who, like Stephen Dedalus, can see a story as it unfolds. To involve them in this creative process, we respond to their inherent love of stories and we tap the hidden wealth of stories within each of them.

As we begin, we tell our students that they are all storytellers and that their stories will become part of our text. They protest, of course, claiming "I don't have anything to say" or "Nothing ever happens to me" or "My life is boring." We dismiss these comments by assuring them they are on the threshold of discovering some startling revelations about every person in the class, including the teacher. At this point they don't really believe us, but in their hearts they hope they are wrong. After all, everyone loves a good story, especially about people we know.

While the class is still considering our outrageous promise, we pass around a small bag containing colored squares of paper. Each student reaches in and takes a square, wanting to know what this is all about. The answer becomes obvious as three students hold up purple squares, three others red, three yellow, and so forth, depending on the number of students in the class. We instruct the "purple people" to sit together, the "red people" to do the same, and so on through the colors. Then we give each group the following list:

Characters: a landlady, between 45 and 50 years old
               Billy Weaver, a 17-year-old boy

Place:	a bed-and-breakfast (boarding house) in Bath, a large city in England
Things:	the guest register
	a glowing hearth
	a very quiet dachshund
	a parrot in a cage

After answering questions about what a hearth, a dachshund, and a bed-and-breakfast are, we tell each color group to create a story about these characters in this specific place and to make each of the things on the list important to the story.

Because they are working in groups of three, our disenchanted students are willing to try, at least, to create a story. Immediately, however, they realize what is missing from the list: any suggestion of a plot line.

"What's this story supposed to be about?" they ask. "That's what you must decide," we answer. "You create the plot."

Some groans may ensue, but we ignore them and assure our students they can invent as intriguing a plot as anyone else—maybe even better.

As they begin to discuss possible scenarios, we go from group to group, listening and answering questions, but being careful not to offer story ideas or suggest criticism of what we overhear. Gradually plot lines begin to unfold. As they do, we caution each group to make sure that one of them records what they've talked about. When 10 minutes are left in the period, we ask each group's recorder to read back what has been created thus far and to make some additional notes as to where they want to go next with the story. We collect what they have written, promising to return the materials at the next class period. In the meantime we review each group's notes to see what has been created and to ensure their safekeeping for further development.

At our next meeting students in the groups are usually eager to get back to work on their stories; some even come to class with additional ideas with which to impress their group's members. We give them time to work, telling them to complete their stories by the end of the period. We assure them that the roughness of the narratives will not count against them, that we want only a general story idea from each group to share with the class. The groups have already become proprietary about their stories, but now that an element of competition has been added, they focus their attention on completing the scenarios. At the end of the period we collect the materials, mainly for safekeeping, and instruct them to bring journals (preferably 8-by-10-inch spiral notebooks) to every class period from now on.

The day we share the story ideas is fun for everyone, in part because each student has contributed something to the plot line and because the class is interested in each group's story. We offer general praise, pointing out at least one specific element in each story idea to compliment. Along the way students comment on the difficulty of including all the "things" in their scenarios. Their complaints provide us with the opportunity to introduce the story from which we extracted these elements, Roald Dahl's "The Landlady." We read the story aloud to the class, whose attention is focused on Dahl's plot and his presentation of the characters and incorporation of the "things." We dramatize the story as we read to help our listeners "see" the glowing hearth, the dachshund, and the caged parrot as Dahl describes them. Their ironic significance gradually becomes clear. At the end our students almost all agree that the story is weird, that events like that don't happen in real life, and that Dahl didn't create a believable story. Some students say they prefer their own versions of the story. We encourage the discussion. Already our students are talking like writers, raising issues of credibility and technique. Even though they may not realize what they are doing, they have entered into a creative interaction between themselves and the writer.

At this point we ask them to write their reactions to the story in their journals, assuring them that there are no right or wrong reactions, only their personal responses based on their reading of the text. To provide a context for their responses to "The Landlady" and other stories they will be reading, we give them copies of "Questions for Responding to Stories" to staple in their journals:

1. What is your first reaction to the story? Briefly describe your emotional response to the story, that is, how the story makes you feel.
2. What are the major events in the story?
3. Upon what did you focus most intently as you read—What word, phrase, image, or idea?
4. What did you have the most difficulty understanding?
5. What other literary work (poem, play, film, etc.) does this story call to mind? What connections do you see between the two?
6. Would you recommend this story to someone? Why or why not? Compare your responses to those of someone else in the class.
7. How do your responses compare to those of someone else in the class?

To get our students started, we model the assignment by sharing our own responses to "The Landlady." In response to Question 1 Ruth tells her class that she knew from the first few pages that something extraordinary would happen; she cites specific references and explains that Dahl was preparing his reader for the preternatural. Marcia tells her class in response to Question 4 that it took her a while to realize what the strange smells Billy Weaver kept noticing had in common; but when she realized all the smells suggested formaldehyde, she knew what was going to happen. Ruth says this story reminds her of the play *Arsenic and Old Lace,* in which two dotty old ladies systematically poison elderly gentlemen boarders with elderberry wine laced with arsenic. Because of the bizarre nature of the story, Marcia is reminded of *Charley and the Chocolate Factory* also by Roald Dahl, who devises some outlandish accidents to get rid of obnoxious children.

After we model our responses, the students write their reactions in their journals. Rich compares his reactions to the story with Ruth's; he says he had missed the significance of the odd smells and the familiar-sounding names Billy saw in the guest register and thus wasn't prepared for the story's ending. He also confesses that he likes his group's story idea better than Dahl's. Ruth assures him that this is allowed. Amy compares her reactions with Marcia's, saying she is having trouble imagining anyone having a bunch of stuffed bodies around the house, as the landlady did. "Really sick," she exclaims.

By the end of our work on "The Landlady" our students are beginning to feel comfortable talking about stories and are ready for another one. What we choosevaries from class to class, depending on our students' language abilities, maturity level, and interests. The primary criterion at this point, however, is that the story be accessible to our students, not so much in terms of reading level, but in its plot and characters. Our goals here are twofold: to destroy the myth that only English teachers and textbook editors know a story's "real meaning," which is deliberately hidden from ordinary folks; and to enable our students to become active readers who can visualize a narrative and respond to it in a personal way. Therefore, no matter what story we select, we connect an aspect of it to something in our students' lives about which they write. For this reason and because of our disenchanted students' general resistance to dated language, we focus our attention on contemporary fiction.

Because many of our students have very little experience with critical reading, we begin with clearly plotted stories, such as "Ah Love, Ah Me" by Max Steele. Even though this piece was written some years ago, the situation has an immediacy for our students. We read the story aloud because we want everyone in the class engaged with the efforts of a teenage boy trying to get up enough nerve to ask a popular girl to go to the movies with him. He finally gets the date, and after the movie he takes her to the drugstore for a soda. That's when the trouble begins. We read up to the climactic part of the story and then stop. "Come on, finish the story," our students insist. "Tell us what happened."

But we don't. Instead we ask them to complete it, describing what they think would logically happen. To get them started, we remind them of what they already know of the characters, emphasizing that plot action always develops from character. Based on what we know about a person, we can predict what he or she will do in a given situation. To make the writing more comfortable for our students, we encourage them to confer with their color group-mates.

The best part of this exercise is the sharing of the various story endings. Predictably, some students decline to read theirs aloud, and that's acceptable; we always have enough students willing to share their work to keep the class lively. After all, there's no threat from the teacher here, only praise for what they do well.

After their story endings are read, we read Max Steele's version. This time students are even more responsive in their comparisons of the writer's version and theirs. Of course, what they are doing is identifying the elements of a logical plot developing from characterization.

We instruct our students to write a response to this story in their journals. We write, too, but this time not to model the activity, only to share the writing time, which we have come to realize is also a modeling process: that of disciplined, focused writing.

To engage our students in Charles Baxter's story "Gryphon," we ask our students to recall the most unforgettable teacher they ever had. To stimulate their thinking, we tell about one of our unforgettable teachers. Ruth says she will never forget Mrs. Schuenberger, her fourth-grade teacher. She was a heavy-set, large-boned woman who had only two dresses—at least as Ruth remembers—each of which was black rayon, short-sleeved, and resplendent with huge red roses. And she wore black "old-lady" shoes, the ones with laces and thick heels. Her hair was iron gray, cut in a short bob; she wore no makeup and no jewelry, except for a large wristwatch strapped onto her heavy, hairy arm. Ruth says she wasn't very attractive, but she had kind eyes, a friendly smile, and infinite patience with all kinds of kids.

As Ruth shares her memories of Mrs. Schuenberger, she remembers even more details. "This is what happens," she tells the class, "as we begin to exercise our memories. Now you write in your journal about an unforgettable teacher."

They write for 10—15 minutes. Then we ask them to share with the class what they have written. It never fails that more than one student will remember the same teacher; then they compare notes, adding to the accumulation of details each has. This sharing period always generates much laughter and some surprises as well.

Now students are ready for "Gryphon," a story about a substitute teacher. We like this one because it's told in the first person, from the perspective of a nine-year-old, and is rich in dialogue. Again we read the story aloud, but this time we get help from the class. To dramatize the action, we assign students who are good readers to assume parts. We read the narrative, unless we have a student who is a strong reader and is willing to take on the task.

After the reading, students comment on Miss Ferenczi, the substitute teacher, and the children's reactions to her, especially those of the narrator. We talk about his being a child. Obviously a nine-year-old has not written the story, but we see the events from his perspective. We ask how that affects the storytelling. Our students are not sure. So we ask them to go back to their journals and look at their remembrances of a particular teacher. "If you wrote about an elementary school teacher, what would happen if you told your story from the perspective of yourself as a child? Would you have as much understanding of the teacher or the situation?"

We discuss the possibilities, referring periodically to Baxter's story to see what he had revealed about the boy's feelings and insights. As we look again at the story, we also consider the rich dialogue. We ask, "What does the dialogue do for you as you read this story—or any story, for that matter?" Our students recognize that dialogue can help create an image of a character and keep the reader interested in the story.

We ask them to add dialogue to their stories about a teacher and, if they wish, to include some more characters. "I can't remember what anybody said," a student may complain. We tell them to remember the general ideas of what was said and then to create the dialogue from that. We assure them that we are not looking for the actual facts but the story of their experience. And we tell them that dialogue will help their readers see it for themselves, just as Baxter's dialogue helps us see his story.

This first story-writing experience is relatively easy for most students. After all, they are working from their own experiences, Baxter's story provides a lively model of first-person narrative rich in dialogue, and they already know they are writing for an appreciative audience: their classmates and teacher. The day the stories are to be read, we ask for volunteers. Meghan was eager to read her story, which she revised and edited for her portfolio (more on portfolios later):

The Day the Ducks Mooed

My first grade teacher, Mrs. Faigle, was probably in her mid-30's. She had kind of dirty blonde hair and looked very tall from where I was. One day she had us doing some math problems. Somehow the math was associated with farm animals. I wasn't understanding it. I think she knew because when she would call on me, I would never know the answer.

"Meghan, how many ducks do you see?" she asked in a tone of voice that told me she didn't expect me to know the answer.

"Four," I replied.

"What sounds do ducks make, Meghan?" I couldn't figure out why she asked me that.

"They moo, Mrs. Faigle," I told her. I knew better, but that's what I said, so I was stuck with it.

"Whoever told you a thing like that?"

"My mother did." I lied.

"Well, they quack." When she said that, the whole class looked at me like I was crazy.

"Ducks don't moo dummy," sneered Mike DeVito, the class wiseass.

Mrs. Faigle didn't seem to appreciate Mike's comments. "Don't you ever speak to anyone that way, young man," she said.

Michael had this smirk on his face and said, "Well, I know Meghan's wrong."

Kay, the brain in the class, raised her hand and said, "Mrs. Faigle, I know Ducks quack because I heard a duck quack once in a lake. Cows moo."

Just then we heard a knock on the door.

"Come in," Mrs. Faigle said.

The door opened and the principal walked in. "Good morning class," he said.

"Good morning Mr. Integra," we responded in unison. We always greeted him that way.

"What are we learning today?" he asked.

Mike DeVito raised his hand and smiled at me. "That ducks moo!"

"Ducks don't moo, Mr. DeVito. Who would ever tell you something like that?"

"Meghan did. She says ducks moo. Isn't she stupid?"

Mr. Integra seemed very upset with Michael because he had called me stupid, but I didn't care. I liked thinking Ducks could moo.

We hear stories about teachers who, according to the storytellers, victimize their children or are terrorized by them, who have made children hate school or love it, who have intimidated children or made them feel good about themselves. But for the most part, what we hear is our students beginning to write with an awareness of the writer's craft nurtured by their reading. To build on this achievement, we review what we have learned about point of view and perspective from "Gryphon" and our own writing. To reinforce the learning, we read another story detailing childhood experiences. Again, what we choose from among the many superbly crafted stories available depends on the class. However, we do like stories from Jean Stafford's Bad Characters, particularly the title story and "The Scarlet Letter." ("Two Kinds" and "Four Directions" from Amy Tan's The Joy Luck Club also work well.) Both of these pieces are told by an iconoclastic eleven-year-old named Emily Vanderpool. Emily is always in trouble, usually self-generated, at school and with her family, but she's an appealing person who gets caught up by circumstance,—actually, not unlike many of our disenchanted students—which is why students respond postively to her.

Stafford's stories offer us an opportunity to elaborate on the shared reading we have been doing in class. After the first reading of either story we reform the color groups. Each group is asked to select one episode from the story to dramatize. For example, in "Bad Characters" a group may choose Emily's first encounter with Lottie Jump or the expedition to Woolworth's or any number of other scenes.

The same is true for "The Scarlet Letter." A group may choose Emily's visit to Virgil Meade's house or her confrontation with her teacher, among others.

To prepare these dramatized vignettes, each group must carefully reread its selected section and translate the narrative into dialogue. That there's already a great deal of dialogue in the story makes this task easier. If the scene requires more than three characters, students from one group may call upon someone from another group to take a part during the presentation.

The point of this activity is to give our students experience in translating narrative into dialogue, a skill they need to expand their journal entries into stories and to enable them to "see" the story. Many of our disengaged students have had limited experiences as young children in being read to and in developing the ability to visualize a story. Nurtured on television, they have not had to exercise their imagination; for them the action has been prepackaged and the ideas predigested. As a result, their ability to visualize, to imagine, even to fantasize has been stunted. Therefore, much of what we do with our students is designed to stimulate their imaginations and, we believe, enrich their lives.

Once the dramatizations and the journal responses to thestories are completed, we acknowledge the advantages of the first-person point of view but suggest that sometimes writers need more distance between themselves and the characters, especially if they decide to fictionalize an incident. "What do you mean?" they ask. And so we explain by sharing with them incidents from our own lives. They are interested inour stories, especially when we tell about experiences we had as children and teenagers—"in the olden days," they say. Ruth tells a story about a time she had accepted a date with a boy she didn't particularly like and was later asked to a party by another boy, one whom she preferred. She knew she should honor the first invitation, but instead she lied to him, telling him she was sick, so she could accept the second invitation. Ruth goes into some detail about her conflicting feelings of guilt and pleasure, describing the elaborate lie inflicted on the first boy and the excitement she felt getting ready for her date with the second boy. All of these details are preparation for her arrival at the party, where she walked right into the boy to whom she had lied.

"What did you do?" the students ask. "What did the first guy say to you?" and "What about the second guy? What did he think?"

Ruth answers the questions by finishing her story. Then she asks, "How much of that story was fact and how much was fiction?" Obviously they don't know. She tells them that part of the story, specifically where she ran into the first boy at the party, was fiction. But, she says, "it doesn't matter because I was creating a story about feelings. The imagined confrontation at the party helped to do that. However, in writing this story, I will have an easier time with the fictionalized part if I write in the third person. I have difficulty inventing things about myself." She adds, "Besides, it's not a very flattering picture of me," which, paradoxically, is what engages her students: she has revealed something personal about herself, especially her feelings when she was a young teenager in "the olden days."

Having told a personal story to be written from the perspective of someone else, we invite our students to examine a third-person narrative. Manuel Rojas's "The Glass of Milk" describes the struggle for survival of a very hungry boy alone and broke in a seaport town. ("Lullaby" by Leslie Silko is an appropriate alternative.) Students read the story aloud, one student reading the narration and others assuming parts. Because the dialogue is realistic and the narrative is rich in sensory details, the story comes vividly to life. At the end of the reading we ask our students why they think Rojas wrote the story in the third person. They offer several reasons, all acceptable. We tell our students that a story written in the first person can be completely fictional; the narrator could be an invention of the author's imagination, which, in fact, is the case with Jean Stafford's Emily Vanderpool. However, we believe Emily must be an extention of her creator because all characterizations are rooted in their creators' personalities and experiences.

But we move on to something else: the sensory details. We ask our students to write down what words, phrases, and images from the story stand out in their memories as they recall the story they have just read. "Hungry," they say, "exhausted," "dizzy," "a burning in the pit of his stomach," "the glass of milk," "he cried and cried," and "the woman caressing his head." If our students haven't offered it, we add, "Then the weariness . . . began to invade his legs in a slow itching, and he sat down . . . The harbor lights extended over the water in a reddish and golden furrow, rippling softly . . . He felt alive, nothing more."

The power of these images lies in their appeal to the senses. Even if we have never had a burning in our insides from hunger and despair, Rojas makes us experience something of what the boy in the story felt because we can identify with his ability to see, smell, hear, taste, and touch. Joseph Conrad stated that it was the writer's responsibility to engage his reader in the sensory experiences of a character. He said, "My task . . . is by the power of the written word to make you hear, to make you feel . . . to make you see. That—and no more, and it is everything."

We want our students to enable their readers to hear, feel, see, and experience, so we ask them to tell us about a time they almost died. At first some students may protest, claiming they never had a near-death experience, but we insist they have, expanding the assignment metaphorically to include a time they almost "died" of embarrassment, humiliation, shame, regret, fear, shyness, disappointment, laughter, or, of course, from love. We model the assignment by sharing an example from our own lives. Marcia tells about the time she almost died of appendicitis.

She was seven years old and with her family was living temporarily with friends. Because she had to sleep in a room with their friends' children, her mother had instructed her to be very quiet, never to disturb anyone at night. One night, though, she was awakened by a terrible pain in her stomach. She wanted to cry out for her mother, but she remembered her mother's warning not to disturb anyone in the house for any reason. Although she wanted to scream, she was afraid of making her mother angry. So she stifled her cries of pain by turning her face into her pillow. Finally, after what seemed like hours of suffering, Marcia could tolerate the pain no longer and made her way down the long, dark hallway to the living room, where her parents were sleeping. Her mother was sympathetic but reluctant to disturb a doctor in the middle of the night, even though Marcia's cold body was drenched with sweat. Instead she put a heavy rubber hot-water bottle on Marcia's stomach (the worst thing she could have done), sponged her body with rubbing alcohol, and waited for a more respectable time of day to call the doctor, who told her to take her child immediately to the nearest hospital. By the time Marcia got there, she was screaming in agony. And for good reason: Her appendix was about to burst. Later the doctor said that another few minutes delay could have cost Marcia her life.

What makes Marcia's story effective is that she involves us in her experience through sensory appeals. We can hear her muffled cries of pain, touch her clammy body, smell the rubbing alcohol, feel the heat from the hot-water bottle, and see her struggling down the darkened hallway to her mother's bed.

Writer Doris Lessing does much the same thing in her story "Through the Tunnel." (Sometimes we use "Hunger" from Black Boy by Richard Wright.) This compelling third-person narrative focuses on a young boy, Jerry, on vacation at the seashore. Jerry develops a casual relationship with some older boys and swims with them every day, but they desert him by swimming through a natural undersea tunnel. Desperate to keep up, he realizes he must find the tunnel and then be able to hold his breath long enough to swim through it. Lessing enables us to identify with the boy's struggle by letting us see, smell, taste, touch, and hear his experiences, especially his attempt to swim through the tunnel.

Our students get caught up in this story as we read it aloud, sharing the responsibility with willing students. At the end we ask them how the story made them feel, physically. "Breathless," they say, "but good, too, because the boy succeeded."

"Did you think he would?" we ask.

Some are convinced he would drown, others aren't sure, but they all agree that author Doris Lessing makes her readers feel like they are going through the experience with Jerry. We confirm what they already know: that Lessing's powerful appeal to our senses has made the story come alive for us; she has shown us her story. To reinforce their sensitivity to sensory appeals, we have our students work in their groups to find specific sensory images from the story. As they work together, we move about the room, sitting in on groups that need help, offering a few suggestions, and generally reviewing their work. Our students record "The roof was sharp and pained his back. He pulled himself along with his hands—fast, fast—and used his legs as levers . . . He was without light and the water seemed to press upon him with the weight of rock . . . his head was pulsing...swelling, his lungs cracking . . ." and finally, "He drifted to the surface, his face turned up to the air. He was gasping . . . He could see nothing but a red-veined, clotted dark. His nose was bleeding, and the blood had filled the goggles."

The power of Lessing's writing is compelling. We use it to inspire our students to review and revise their stories of a time they almost died. Tina, a talented young writer, developed her journal entry about a time she almost died from grief into a fictional story about a literal death. Notice the skill with which she appeals to her reader's senses:

> [O]ne day she went swimming and never came back. There was no body. We held a service by the ocean with a small box of sea-glass standing in for my mother. Over the course of a lifetime she had collected hundreds of the small pieces of glass rubbed smooth by the tumbling of the ocean. The sun was blistering that day, and it seemed hotter beating against our dark clothing. I remember how the stones caught the light and then threw it back, like so many winking eyes mocking our black-cloaked sorrow, flaunting their brightness in silent flirtations. Overhead flew the ever-present sea gulls, their screeches filtering down through the smothering heat.

Tina's story, of which we have included only a paragraph, and Lessing's "The Tunnel" provide us the opportunity to look at stories not just as a literal telling of events and feelings, but as implied representations of something else—an idea, a theme—that reveals some insight into our human condition. For example, the tun-nel could represent any challenging experience a person may have to face in order to achieve a goal; the seashore memorial for the mother could represent our griefs for the many necessary losses, the little "deaths," we must face throughout our lives.

We let rest for a moment the idea of a story implying something much greater than what it literally says and ask our students to empty the contents of their pockets and handbags onto their desks. Because this request is so unexpected, they comply, curious about what's on each student's desk, laughing and commenting about the wide variety of stuff everyone carries around. Of course we empty the contents of our handbags too.

When the initial interest begins to wane, we ask each student to consider carefully what she or he carries around. "What does that collection of stuff say about you?" Using our own collections to model the activity, we examine our belongings and offer some general comments. For example, Ruth carries a small personal phone directory because, she explains, "I have trouble remembering numbers. I'm a real 'number-phobe.' It started with my difficulty in math, which I hated. I guess subconsciously I associate numbers with math class, so I have to write them down to remember them and look them up when I have to use them."

We ask our students to do what Ruth did, to select one thing from their collections and to tell, in their journals, what significance that item has or what it reveals about the person who carries it.

The journal writing is a prelude to our reading another story, one that is longer and more complicated than others we have read. For this purpose we like "The Things They Carried" by Tim O'Brien. This story is set in Vietnam during the war. (Many of our students have fathers or other relatives who served in Vietnam, which alone enhances the story's appeal.) O'Brien has his readers follow along with a platoon of young soldiers—or grunts, as they are called— and their lieutenant on a search-and-destroy mission. Each of them carries a 15–20 pound burden: weapons, supplies, rations, and personal belongings. The author meticulously lists these real objects and then subtly includes all the abstract things, the hopes, dreams, terrors, griefs, and so on that each soldier also carries. We begin reading this story aloud, but then we give our students time for silent reading, for this is a very personal story that needs to be internalized individually.

After the reading, students want to talk about the personal "baggage" of the soldiers, especially that of Lieutenant Cross, who carries an elaborate fantasy of a relationship with a girl named Martha. Just touching her photograph transports him into the world of romantic possibilities. Later this image of love and longing is superseded by the burden of guilt and shame. So powerful is O'Brien's writing that our students can indeed hear, feel, and, above all, see the story.

After our discussions and responses to "The Things They Carried," we ask our students to go back to their journal entries describing one thing they carry that has significance in their lives. With O'Brien's story in mind, we ask them to develop that journal entry into a personal narrative describing the emotional thing they carry, which may or may not be represented by an object they carry.

Ruth models the process by telling them that something she carries, the memory of her father, is not represented by the objects in her handbag. However, it is such an important part of her emotional life that she will write about it anyway. She plans her writing on the board, jotting down ideas, rearranging details, and experimenting with words. As she writes, she thinks out loud, sharing the composing process with her students. By the time she's filled the board, she's ready to get to the writing of a first draft, at which point she and her students work independently.

For most students, this writing assignment opens doors for them to release strong emotions. Certainly this was true for Adam, who was able to find words to express some powerful emotions:

The Things I Carry

I carry many things with me everyday: my keys, my wallet with pictures of my friends in it, and my necklace. But along with these material things I carry a feeling of hurt, which just won't go away.

This feeling started back in 9th grade when I found out my father was embezzeling money from his firm. I don't think I can ever forgive him for what he did, at least not any time soon. He's sitting in prison now where he has a chance to think about what he did to our family.

Ever since I found out what my father had done, I have been hurt, and the more I've thought about it, the more hurt I've become. At first, just my family knew what had happened, then the whole town knew because the story was in the papers. I couldn't believe this was happening to me, but it was. Now I'm weighted down with this awful feeling of pain that never goes away.

At times I think I've put it out of my head, but then something will remind me of it all, like the phone ringing. Every once in a while, when I pick up the receiver, a voice will say, "I have a collect call from Arthur at the correctional facility, will you accept the charges?" Not once have I answered that question. I always throw the phone to my mother and walk out of the room.

Maybe some day I'll feel different. Maybe some day I won't hurt anymore. But not now, not yet.

Sandor found in this assignment an opportunity to tell about a personal epiphany.

A Little Bit of Light

I don't carry around many material things, and they are insignificant anyway. But I do carry a a lot of guilt for something I did in my younger year. I used to beat up little kids and humiliate them. I hate to admit it, but I enjoyed doing it, I felt powerful. Now I can't believe how evil that was.

The revelation of my wicked behavior came to me at an unlikely place. I was walking to see my brother at work, when I passed a playground where three boys were beating up on one other little kid. They were calling him names, kicking sand in his face, punching him, and spitting at him. They were totally humiliating him. He looked at me, his eyes crying for help. I ran up and chased the boys away; one of them laughed as he left.

I pulled the little kid up. He felt like a sack of potatoes. He clamped his hands around my waist and dug his face into my side and cried. I wanted to push him away, but I couldn't find the strength. I looked at him. His clothes and face were dirty and I could tell he was in pain. It did not seem to be so much physical pain, except for his swollen lips, because he was not terribly bruised and bloody. Between choking sobs, he told me he was afraid to tell his father what had happened to him because he would think he was a coward, and he did not want his mother to see him all beat up like this. Obviously, the emotional torment the boys had caused him was far greater than any physical abuse inflicted on him.

There wasn't any more I could do for him, so I pushed him away from me and told him to go home. He walked with his head down and the shoulders slumped; I knew he carried a great burden. So did I.

Guilt washed over me after he left. I thought of the pain I had inflicted on others. I also thought of how I had enjoyed doing it. I thought I was going to cry I felt so bad. That's when I began to realize the effects of senseless violence. Sometime later, two of my friends were about to get in a fight. One was ready to kill; I could see it in his eyes. In the eyes of the other I saw fear and pain, just like in the little kid's. So I stopped the fight. It felt good, like I had saved both of them and myself.

I guess sometimes there is justification for violence, but to fight to humiliate your opponent or to bully another is totally wrong and unjust. I still carry a burden of guilt for past action, but I now know better and will continue to try to ease my burden by stopping fights whenever I can.

When our students have completed revising their stories, many of them want to share them with the class. This desire surprises us because of the very personal nature of these narratives; however, in many instances the writing has been cathartic, and so the writers want to share their experiences with classmates. Besides, sharing in our classes is never threatening to their self-esteem.

"The Things They Carry" emphasizes the power of symbols in storytelling. To reinforce this awareness, we select a story whose meaning is conveyed through a symbol. Walter Van Tilburg Clark's "Portable Phonograph" serves this purpose very well. As the title suggests, a phonograph is the dominant symbol in this powerful allegory of man's paradoxical power to create that which is spiritually ennobling and at the same time to destroy the earth and all that exists upon it.

Because Clark implies a great deal, only alluding to what has happened before the story begins, we ask our students, after we have read the story aloud, to speculate about what has caused the "weed-grown cavities," "the rutted remains of a road," "the tangled and multiple barbed wire of the bleak landscape." Without any prompting, the students speculate that the land has been bombed, probably by atomic bombs, and that only a remnant of the human race is struggling to survive. Whether the remnant makes it is doubtful, considering the physical conditions after the holocaust and what Clark suggests about the nature of the men themselves. Even the doctor who shares his phonograph and books with the others goes to bed with his hand holding "the comfortable piece of lead pipe," ready for an attack.

In our discussion of what has preceded the story, we have identified other things besides the phonograph that seem to have symbolic significance. We ask students to identify the symbols in Clark's story and to speculate as to their meanings. We get the color groups started thinking about things in the story other than the phonograph that could have symbolic meaning, for example, the setting itself. It's a bitterly cold winter, the trees are bare, the creek is frozen, and wolves are howling. "Besides setting a mood, what does this lifeless landscape suggest to you?" we ask. We don't want an immediate answer, nor are we looking for any one "right" answer; we ask the question only to stimulate each group's thinking.

A quilt becomes a powerful symbol in Alice Walker's mythic story "Everyday Use." The quilt is representative of a history, a way of life, a culture that has been rejected by a young woman in the story who believes her education has taken her beyond the quaint mores of her rural Southern black heritage.

Walker contrasts the ingenuous honesty of Maggie and her mother with the condescending pretentiousness of the educated Dee. Dee is ashamed of the "large, big-boned woman with rough, man-working hands," and the "dingy grey boards" of the tiny three-room house. She sees value in the household objects only as relics to be displayed in her modern apartment. She wants the quilt, handmade of "scraps of dresses Grandma Dee had worn fifty and more years ago. Bits and pieces of Grandpa Jarrell's Paisley's shirts . . . and Great Grandpa Ezra's uniform that he wore in the Civil War," just to hang on a wall.

Again we ask students to reconvene their color groups to look more closely at the symbolic significance of the quilt as it reflects the differing social attitudes of Dee, Maggie, and Mama, the narrator. Our students note particularly Dee's affectation of an African name in her search for an identity apart from her humble origin and Maggie's appreciation of the intrinsic value of the heritage repre-sented by grandma's quilts. However, our students need some guidance to ascertain the irony of Dee's charge that Maggie and her mother don't understand their heritage when in truth it is Dee—or Wangeroo, as she insists on being called—who is ignorant of the value of her past.

After our students have discussed these stories, focusing particularly on symbols to convey ideas, and have completed their reader response entries in their journals, we ask them to remember a journey they have taken, not just any journey, but one that has some special, symbolic meaning in their lives. The journey may have been very short in actual number of miles traveled and time spent, but in terms of the effect on them it should be considerable.

Marcia models the exercise by telling about her journey from disaster. When she was a small child, she saw a playmate knocked off his bicycle and dragged under a pickup truck. She stared at the scene momentarily, terrified by what had happened and repulsed by the stench of burning rubber. All she could do was run home as fast as she could, not for help for the boy, but to get away from the horror, to get to safety, away from the street where pain and death can reach out even to children.

When the journal entries are written, we introduce another story, "A Worn Path," by one of our favorite writers, Eudora Welty. This story, perhaps more effectively than any other we have read, incorporates all the elements of story-telling that our students have considered in their reading and writing.

We read the story to the class, not sharing the responsibility this time because we want our students to hear the dialect of the old woman as she journeys on a "worn path" to get medicine for her grandson, to see the piney woods through which she travels, to touch the thorny bush that entraps her, to taste the sweet spring water she drinks, to smell cold, dried corn husks that whirl about her skirt, and most of all to feel the dignity and abiding love of the old woman. This story, rich in characterization, language, and allusion, is universal in its mythic depiction of courage and self-sacrifice.

When our students have completed their journal responses to the story (they need no prompting from the teachers), we ask them to review the journal entries about their personal journey, comparing their presentations of setting, characters, dialogue, symbol, and theme with that of Eudora Welty in "A Worn

Path." They conclude about their personal entries what we conclude about ours: that they need a great deal of hard work before they become stories.

And so the task begins. For this effort we move to the computer lab, where the cycle of writing and revising is best facilitated. We help each other, and we also let the writers whose stories we have read instruct us.

The results are always exciting to read. Some stories are "slices of life"; others are rich in fantasy. We enjoy them all.

Now we ask our students to re-form their color groups and select one of the stories to dramatize for a video production. The students determine the criteria for selecting one of the three stories: that it is clearly visualized, has interesting characters, and has lots of dialogue. They have already had some experience dramatizing narrative (remember the dramatizations of Jean Stafford's stories), so they set to work preparing a script.

Once the script is complete, we give them video storyboard forms on which they plan their shots to coordinate the action, dialogue, sound effects, and music, if they choose to use it. (See page 93, and review Chapter 6 on the making of poetry videos.)

On the days the videos are presented, we invite the principal and students from one or two other classes to watch. They are given a listing of all the productions and are asked to rank them on a scale of 1 through 10. The three productions with the highest scores win prizes, presented by the principal. We invite a reporter from the school newspaper to get the story and photograph the winners on Awards Day.

As exciting and spirit-boosting as the video productions might be—especially because they afford students who are not necessarily successful as writers form to shine—they do not always reward the most thoughtfully conceived and best-written stories. For these awards we let the class make the selections. After all, they now recognize the elements of a well-written story and invariably acknowledge the classmates who are the most accomplished writers. Frank Borrelli's story, " Staying Alive," is one of those class winners:

> I was standing at my locker flipping through my notebook looking for a lost English essay when I heard the musical voice of an angel say, "Hey Barnaby, I want to talk to you."
>
> Turning to face her, I gasped. Those icy blue eyes, that golden hair, the crimson lips! I dropped my notebook; paper went scattering across the floor. It didn't matter, nothing mattered. Oilvia was talking to me! If only she would sing more beautiful music to me. She did.
>
> "Stop drooling you jerk and listen up."
>
> Not quite what I was hoping for, but completely acceptable as far as I was concerned.
>
> "There's going to be a party at Jim's house tonight and I want you to go with me," she said.
>
> Oh blessed miracle! Was she serious? Was she asking me out on a date? I couldn't believe it. The most gorgeous girl in school was asking me out! Then it hit me. Obviously, she had seen beyond my lack of muscle, my thick-

rimmed glasses, my braces, and the fact that most people figure me to be a nerd.

Yes, she has seen me for what I truly am—a Renaissance man, a lover of poetry, theatre, and the arts. This woman had class.

"I would be greatly honored to accompany you to Jim's social gathering," I answered.

She sighed and rolled her eyes to the sky, no doubt thanking God that I had accepted her gracious invitation. Rejection is a hard thing to deal with. I felt good not having let her down.

"Listen Barnaby," she said, jabbing a finger into my chest. (It hurt, but I didn't mind. She was nervous and it occurred to me that a man as dashing as I am could be an intimidating presence to those of the female gender. I tried to act casual.) "Don't get any crazy ideas. The only reason I am taking you is because my friends and I made a bet that I could change you into a man for at least one night." She seemd to survey me for a moment. "And no matter how bad the odds are, I'm going to give it my best shot." With that she handed me a piece of paper, whirled around, and strode off down the hallway.

A bet? She asked me on account of a bet? My heart stopped beating. It really did. I put a hand on my chest, and I couldn't feel a beat. I couldn't breathe. Quickly I reached my hand into my pocket, withdrew my anti-asthma bottle and shoved it into my mouth. In a moment I could breathe again. That was close. Dying in a school corridor would have been an awful way to go. I reminded myself to take my pills.

Almost instantly I was back to the reality of Olivia, the date, the bet. I analyzed the situation. "So, she thinks I'm not a man," I said. Then for the first time it occurred to me that perhaps her feelings for me were not sincere. It was hard to believe. In fact, I didn't believe it. I knew that beneath that body a goddess would envy, and any god or man would desire, there must be an equally beautiful heart. And I, Barnabus Stovesitter, was going to find it.

With renewed confidence, I looked at the paper Olivia had handed me. It said to pick her up at eight o'clock sharp, or else not to show up at all. "Ah!" I said to myself, "I admire punctuality in a girl. Where there's a watch there's a way, I always say. Be prepared Miss Olivia Newair, for tonight at the stroke of eight, you will be swept off your feet!"

After school I rushed home, hurridly did my school work, watched "People's Court" on television, ate dinner, and finally began to get ready for the big night.

Once in my room I closed the door and turned on the stereo. After all, one has to be in the proper mood when dressing for a party. The music was perfect. The Bee Gees were singing the theme song to the movie "Saturday Night Fever." From the closet I retrieved my white two piece suit and my black silk shirt. Putting them on I felt the magic sweeping over me. The music, the greased-back hair, and the bell bottom pants. John Travolta fever was surging through me. I had to dance! I strutted around

the room and stopped in front of the mirror, topping off my electric out-
burst with a twirl that sent my horn-rimmed glasses flying into the wall.

After recovering from a sudden dizzy spell, I picked up my glasses and
looked at my watch. Seven forty-one. Time to move. I grabbed the bou-
quet of flowers from the bed and the heart shaped package of candy from
the dresser and headed out. It was none too soon either since the Bee Gee's
song was ending, and I didn't want to lose the mood. I shut off the stereo, slipped the tape in my pocket, sped out of the house, bidding farewell
to my parents, and grabbed the keys to my Dad's car.

I raced off to Olivia's house and arrived at exactly eight o'clock. She
was standing in the driveway, waiting for me. I got out of the car, said hello
and handed her the flowers and candy.

She took them slowly and seemed to be surveying me again. "You're
not going to the party dressed like that are you?" she asked.

Perhaps I was overdressed. "Why? Is is too fancy?"

"It's ridiculous," she said. "You look like a 1970's reject."

A 70's reject? I sensed she wasn't a Travolta fan. "It's all I have," I pleaded. "Besides, it brings out my charm."

"It brings out your ankles," she sighed. "Those bell bottoms are unbe-
lievable."

Oh boy. She was definitely not a Travolta fan. I was hurt.

For a moment she stood there, silent, then went to the other side of the
car and got in. I got in too, as someone had to drive, and we were off to
the party.

The door to the host's house was half open; the music coming from
beyond it was deafening. Together, Olivia and I strolled in, I shining in
white and she hiding her identity behind flowers and candy.

People were dancing like maniacs to music whose lyrics I could not and
did not want to understand. A few people looked at me and laughed.
Could it be that they were not Travolta fans? I was in shock, as you can
well imagine.

Ten minutes went by as I stood near the punch bowl watching Olivia
talking to some girls. She seemd embarrassed while the other girls laughed
uproariously. Every so often they would look at me and laugh even harder, if that were possible.

I began to realize what was happening. Olivia was losing the bet. She
had not transformed me into hers and her girl friend's idea of a man. And
I knew why. Looking around the room I could see that every man was doing
what I wasn't. Dancing. All of them were flailing around like dying fish. I
could do much better than that. I knew disco!

I looked at the depressed Olivia. I could see that the gleam in her blue
eyes was fading. I would not let that happen. I knew what had to be done.
And I was prepared.

Wading through the tangle of people, I made my way to the stereo. I
hit the eject button and removed the tape. The music stopped and so did
all the dancing people. They just stood there looking at me, probably in

admiration. From my jacket pocket I withdrew my own tape, popped it in the slot, and pressed the play button. I pushed my way to the center of the room and told everyone to give me some space. They look surprised, but they formed a circle around me.

Then the music began. The tune started softly and slowly, then built to a loud but pleasant level. This was my music. This was the Bee Gees! I began to strut around the circle, doing a few complicated twists and turns. I was getting that feeling again, the feeling of purpose, pride, and dignity. I could feel the essence of John Travolta swell within me. I was a free spirit, able to do anything! I attempted a running split. As I went down, I heard it, the sound of fabric being torn apart. My pants had taken the split literally. Worse yet, the pants fit so tight that I hadn't worn any underwear!

The music stopped. The crowd stood silent for moment. Then, simultaneously, the whole lot of them began to laugh. This wasn't quite the response to my dancing I had planned.

To my left, through the crowd, I could see Olivia running out the door. I took off my jacket, wrapped it around my hips, and ran after her through the crowd, which wasn't very difficult since most of them were on the floor in mass hysterics. The swine.

I caught up with Olivia on the front lawn. "Olivia," I said. "You asked me to go to this party with you because of a bet, and I went. I dressed up for you, bought you gifts, chauffered you, and finally, in trying to help you win the bet, made a complete ass of myself in front of people who will heckle me for the rest of my life."

The emotion of the moment was swelling up within me. "For God's sake, woman, what must I do to please you?"

She stood there with her back to me, then slowly turned around and handed over my Bee Gees tape. "I didn't want you to forget it," she said softly, still holding the flowers and candy. She looked at them and back to me. "Come on, Barnaby, let's say you and I go see a movie. I'm not in the mood for a party." And she smiled at me, the most devastatingly beautiful smile I have even seen.

Then I knew I had my goddess pegged right all along.
Not only did she have a heart, she would probably even become a Travolta fan.

Throughout "Show Me a Story" students have been writing responses to what they have read, writing about incidents from their personal histories, and writing stories inspired by their reading. In short, they have been doing a great deal of writing, some of it good, some of it not so good. Along the way we have encouraged and guided their writing, but we have not formally evaluated it. Now—in addition to our written comments and reactions to their writing and checks in the grade book to indicate they've kept up with assignments—they want a grade. To determine an overall grade for each of them, we know, as writers ourselves, that it would be unfair to evaluate every piece of their writing. Therefore, we ask each of them to select the best reader response to a story and to expand one journal entry into a revised, edited, and proofread story. These two pieces, along with their story of a personal journey and the script of the group-produced video, constitute each student's portfolio.

We review with them the criteria we will use for evaluating the portfolios:

The reader responses to the stories should demonstrate thoughtful reading, evidence of specifics from the story, and connections and parallels with other works and their own lives.

The story based on a journal entry expanded into the story of a journey should contain credible characters, a story line that follows a logical progression, dialogue where appropriate, sensory details, and some insight into their own lives.

The script of the video should contain appropriately selected scenes from the story, dialogue from the narrative portions of the story, specific blocking, a set design, and camera instructions.

Students submit their portfolios with an anecdotal self-assessment of their work in which they discuss the reasons for their selections, the process of transforming the journal into a story, and their difficulties and successes with reading, responding to, and writing short stories.

We examine the portfolio, commenting extensively on each piece, but we grade the collection holistically, arriving at a single mark that reflects both effort and achievement on the part of each student.

We began this chapter by declaring our desire for our students to become active readers, able to become so engaged in a story that they become part of a creative interaction with the writer. Obviously we believe that active reading is nurtured by writing, which in turn, prompts more active reading and even more writing. We like to share with our students what William Faulkner told his students: "Read, read, read everything . . . just like a carpenter who works as an apprentice and studies the master . . . You'll absorb it. Then write. If it is good, you'll find out. If it's not, throw it out the window."

In "Show Me a Story" our students have the opportunity to become active readers—apprentices who can see, touch, smell, hear, even taste what they read—and then to turn their reading into part of their own experiences about which they can write. In so doing, our students gain an appreciation for themselves as people who have something worth sharing with other readers and writers. We can think of no better rationale for encouraging our students to become readers who write and writers who read than the satisfaction of that personal accomplishment.

Resources

The following list includes the stories mentioned in this chapter, as well as other stories we have used in "Show Me a Story."

Angelou, Maya. "The Extraction" and "Graduation," from *I Know Why the Caged Bird Sings.* (New York: Random House, 1969).

Baxter, Charles, "Gryphon," from *Best American Short Stories of the Eighties.* (Boston: Houghton Mifflin, 1990).

Brooks, Gwendolyn. "Home," from *The World of Gwendolyn Brooks*. (New York: Harper & Row, 1951).

Clark, Walter Van Tilburg. "The Portable Phonograph," from *The Watchful Gods and Other Stories*. (New York: Random House, 1941).

Dahl, Roald. "The Landlady," from *Kiss, Kiss*. (New York: Knopf, 1959).

Essop, Ahmed. "Noorjehan," from *The Hajji and Other Stories*. (Portsmouth, NH: Ravan Press and Heinemann Educational Books, 1980).

Lessing, Doris. "Through the Tunnel," from *Appreciating Literature*. (New York: Scribner Macmillan, 1984).

Norris, Leslie, "Shaving," from *Appreciating Literature*. (New York: Scribner Macmillan, 1984).

O'Brien, Tim. "The Things They Carried," from *Best American Short Stories of the Eighties*. (Boston: Houghton Mifflin, 1990).

Platero, Juanita, and Siyowin Miller. "Chee's Daughter," from *Appreciating Literature*. (New York: Scribner Macmillan, 1984).

Porter, Katherine Anne. "The Jilting of Granny Weatherall," from *Flowering Judas and Other Stories*. (New York: Harcourt Brace Jovanovich, 1969).

Rojas, Manuel; transl. by Anne Murray and Nancy Farnsworth. "The Glass of Milk," from *From Paragraph to Essay*. (New York: Scribner's, 1950).

Silko, Leslie Marmon. "Lullaby," from *A Story Teller*. (New York: Seaver Books, 1981).

Steele, Max. "Ah Love, Ah Me," from *Stories of Impact* (New York: Harcourt Brace Jovanovich, 1986).

Tan, Amy. "Two Kinds" and "Four Directions," from *The Joy Luck Club*. (New York: Ivy Books, 1990).

Walker, Alice. "Everyday Use," from *In Love and Trouble: Stories of Black Women*. (New York: Harcourt Brace Jovanovich, 1973).

Welty, Eudora. "A Worn Path," from *A Curtain of Green*. (New York: Harcourt Brace Jovanovich, 1969).

Wright Richard. "Hunger," from *Black Boy*. (New York: Harper & Row, 1945).

TRIALS AND TRIBULATIONS

It was the best of times, it was the worst of times, it was the age of wisdom, it was the age of foolishness, it was the epoch of belief, it was the epoch of incredulity, it was the season of Light, it was the season of Darkness, it was the spring of hope, it was the winter of despair, we had everything before us, we had nothing before us, we were all going direct to Heaven, we were all going direct the other way—in short, the period was so far like the present period, that some of its noisiest authorities insisted on its being received, for good or for evil, in the superlative degree of comparison only.

Tale of Two Cities *by Charles Dickens*

Charles Dickens was writing about the last two decades of the eighteenth century, a period he described as the best and the worst of times. Dickens, of course, was writing about the turmoil of revolutionary Europe and the resulting contradictions of a society in flux. No individual could escape the effects of these paradoxes. Like the characters in Dickens's novel, our teenage students lead contradictory lives. At home they are still dependent on their parents and subject to their authority, yet they have more opportunities to make independent choices than ever before. At school their academic lives are controlled by teachers and administrators, but the campus is also the social center of their lives. Their behavior is restricted by school authorities, but it is also determined by their emerging individuality and their choice of peers. In the community their actions are limited by the laws, yet they have more freedom than they have ever had before. Shop merchants are worried about teenagers loitering and shoplifting, yet they welcome them as consumers. In short, our teenage students believe they are living in both the best of times and the worst of times.

We ask our students to reflect on this time in their lives as the best and the worst of times. We model the process with our own experiences. Marcia tells her class that she is living in the best of times right now because her children are grown and independent and she can now concentrate on her husband and herself and travel whenever she feels like it, cook dinner or not as it suits her, and enjoy a freedom she has not felt since her own teenage years. However, she also feels it is the worst of times because she has an empty house and she misses being with her children on a daily basis. Students then write in their journals about this time of their lives being the best and worst of times. They complete their entries for homework.

The next day students share their journals in small groups. Each group selects one to read to the class.

John wrote:

I am having a great time being a teenager. I have my own car and can go where I want when I want. Weekends are the best. We party all the time and no one is on my back about coming home a specific time. I really answer only to myself about the things that matter to me—my friends, where I go, what I do. I like not having any real responsibilities. The only problems I have are the pressures my friends put on me. It's hard staying straight when so many of my friends are into drugs. I know who I am and everything but they really bug me about trying stuff. I wind up being the designated driver all the time too. That can get to be a real drag.

Karen wrote:

Everyone always says the teenage years are the best. I wonder what they're talking about. I worry about everything—what my friends will say, how to dress, if my boyfriend will continue to like me, how to get good grades and get into a good college so I can get a good job, everything. I feel so many pressures. My parents are great but they are always after me to study; they even put this timer on the phone so I can't talk more than ten minutes to anybody. I hate it! Yet there are some good things too. I have a lot more privileges than my younger sister, and I like being able to pick out my own clothes, have a job to earn money for whatever I want, and being able to go out on weekends with Roger without any hassles from my parents.

After we shared these and other journal entires, we listed on the board some of the "trials" a number of students had mentioned in their journals: pressures from parents, school and peers; uncertainty about their futures; conflicts over drug and alcohol use; insecurities about girlfriends and boyfriends; earning enough money for college; restrictions on athletic eligibility based on grades. In particular, many of them mentioned a school proposal making community service a requirement for graduation and the new state regulation on the number of hours teenagers can work.

Because so many of our students were impassioned about the new legislation and the proposed requirement for community service, we decided to have Marcia's class explore the implications of the legislation on their lives and to have Ruth's class explore the issue of community service. Our students had very little specific knowledge about either the new law or the proposed graduation requirement and had formed their opinions based on rumor and fear. To counter misinformation, we made the full texts of both issues available to our students. After they had read the documents, they responded personally in their journals to both.

To help students define their positions, we summarized the details of the law and of the proposal on the board. Marcia wrote the following:

The law states that students may work no more than 28 hours a week during the school year. They cannot work past 10 p.m. on any school night nor can they work more than four hours on a school day.

Ruth wrote:

> Students must volunteer 120 hours of their time to community service in order to graduate from high school.

We placed large signs on each of the four sides of our rooms. Marcia hung the following four signs in her classroom:

> I strongly support the new law restricting student work hours.
>
> I support the new law restricting student work hours.
>
> I strongly oppose the new law restricting student work hours.
>
> I oppose the new law restricting student work hours.

Ruth hung the following four signs in her classroom:

> I strongly support the proposal that 120 hours of community service be required for high school graduation.
>
> I support the proposal that 120 hours of community service be required for high school graduation.
>
> I strongly oppose the proposal that 120 hours of community service be required for high school graduation.
>
> I oppose the proposal that 120 hours of community service be required for high school graduation.

In dealing with these two issues, as we have with others in the past, we allow students a few minutes to consider the signs and then tell them to stand under the one that best reflects their feelings on the issue. Once students have made their selections, they discuss their reasons for their choices in their groups for 5–10 minutes. Then we instruct them to plan an argument to convince people in the other groups to accept their position.

To facilitate this, one member of the group acts as a recorder to present the group's position. While the students are working on their arguments, we circulate among the groups, asking questions to elicit specific details that will support the arguments of each group. As we listen to the arguments, particularly of those groups where students only "agree" or "disagree," we ask why they don't feel strongly about their positions. Often an individual will decide at this point to change groups. Others, however, express understanding of both sides of the argument and for that reason, though they may agree or disagree, want to maintain a slightly more neutral position.

As each group presents its position, we ask a member of the group to record on the board the reasons and the specific details advanced by that group in support of its argument. At the end of each presentation we ask if anyone wants to change positions. Some students switch more than once, to the amusement of the class.

By the end of the presentations we have listed on the board all the details of each group's position on the issue. Now we can begin to determine which arguments are the best supported. Invariably, at least one group supplies *reasons* to support reasons rather than provide specific details as support. For example, one group in Marcia's class argued that the proposal was a good idea because students in high school should concentrate primarily on schoolwork. They claimed that working more than 28 hours a week led to poor grades, made it impossible for students to participate in after-school activities, and took away jobs from adults.

Another group that strongly agreed with the proposal argued that working too many hours interfered with school performance. They claimed that students who worked many hours had to work late at night. By the time they got home, they had no time or energy left to do homework. As a result, they came to school unprepared, causing them to fail tests, to turn in assignments late, even to be late for first period class because they were too tired to get up in the morning. After the second presentation a number of students switched into the "strongly agree" group.

Marcia discussed these two presentations with the class, asking why so many students had been persuaded by the second group. They said that the second presentation had been much more specific. The details—of not having time to do homework, getting to school late, failing tests, not turning in assignments—clearly supported the group's contention that too many hours at after-school jobs could hurt school performance. The first group was less persuasive because it did not develop one reason with specifics; instead it used other reasons (too much work leading to poor grades, not being able to participate in after-school activities, and taking jobs away from adults) to support the idea that students should concentrate primarily on schoolwork. Those students who chose to change sides were persuaded by the more logical, concrete presentation of the second group.

In Ruth's class, too, one group was more persuasive than the other. The group that strongly disagreed with the proposal to require 120 hours of community service to graduate from high school argued that it was unfair to force students to volunteer their time. They said that students don't have enough free time to do volunteer work and that forcing them to do it would cause them to resent the school and the community. They argued that they have to work after school to save money for college; they have to baby-sit for their younger brothers and sisters; they have household chores to do for working parents; and they have hours of homework to do to keep up their grades. Again the second group was so persuas-ive that a number of students switched positions. This exercise points out to students that reasons not supported by specific details are not as persuasive as those developed concretely.

Once students have had the opportunity to formulate an opinion, have a few reasons to support that opinion, and have some details with which to develop those reasons, they are ready to work independently on letters to the appropriate authorities.

Marcia's students wrote to their state representative or senator. Ruth's students wrote to the superintendent of schools and to the president of the board of education. Both of us review with our classes the structure of a persuasive composition. For the introduction we ask the students what information the reader will need in order to understand the purpose of the letter. Students mention the specifics of the situation (the new state law or the school board proposal), their positions on the issue, and their reasons for holding those positions.

At this point we ask students to draft their introductions. Jim, who was in Marcia's class investigating the new state law regulating student work hours, wrote:

> I am very upset about the new state law regulating how many hours students can work at after-school jobs. I understand that I can no longer work more than 28 hours a week and can't work past 10 p.m. on any school night. This is a stupid law. I need to work as much as I can to save money for college. Besides, I learn as much from my after-school job as I do in school. Even worse, you are interfering with my individual freedoms by restricting my working hours.

Doreen, who was in Ruth's class investigating the proposed community requirement, wrote:

> I like the new proposal to require 120 hours of community service for graduation from high school. I think it is time we started thinking about people other than ourselves. Up until this point, we have been very lucky and have enjoyed many things the community offered. We owe something back. Besides, we will benefit personally by helping to make our community a nicer place.

Even though Jim and Doreen needed to do more work on their introductions, we left them as they were for the time being, pointing out what they had done well, which was to state their positions clearly and give good reasons for them. What they needed to do was develop those reasons with specific details. For most students this is the most difficult part of the assignment. To help generate details, we ask them questions. For example, for Jim—who needed to support his first reason, that he required money to go to college—Marcia asked:

> What are some of the difficulties parents can have financing the college education of their children?
>
> How much help could a student reasonably expect to provide as a result of working a job more than 28 hours a week?
>
> What satisfaction might a teenager have from contributing as much as possible to his or her own education?

To help Jim with his second reason, which was that he learned as much on his job as at school, Marcia asked:

> What kinds of jobs can a teenager reasonably expect to get?
>
> What skills can be acquired at such a job?
>
> How does holding a job teach a teenager how to deal better with various kinds of people?

Describe a job you have had or someone you know has had in which you learned something that will help you in the future.

To assist Jim with his final reason, that the legislature has no right to limit the hours a student works, Marcia asked:

Over what part of your time do you think the legislature has a right to make regulations?

Who do you think should have the final say over how you spend your time out of school?

Describe an experience when you have been prevented from doing something that was important to you. How did you feel? Could the legislature's regulation affect you in the same way? What might you do as a result?

Ruth used the same technique to help Doreen find details to support her belief that required community service was an appropriate graduation requirement. For Doreen's first reason, that teenagers need to think about people other than themselves, Ruth asked:

What personal advantages are there for teenager who think about people other than themselves? List them.

What do teenagers learn from helping other people? List what they learn.

How can teenagers use what they learn to benefit themselves in the future? List the benefits.

Think of two specific examples of a teenager helping other people. Maybe these are personal experiences. Describe the experiences and explain the personal advantages: what the teenager may have learned and the benefits to him or her in the future.

For Doreen's second reason, that teenagers owe their communities volunteer time in repayment for the benefits they have received as residents of the community, Ruth asked:

What benefits do teenagers enjoy as residents of your community? List them

What specific volunteer activities can teenagers perform to show their gratitude to the community? List them.

Think of two specific examples of teenagers volunteering their time to community service. These may be personal experiences. Describe these examples in detail and explain the specific activities and benefits.

For Doreen's third reason, that teenagers will become better citizens and more responsive to the needs of others by volunteering, Ruth asked:

What are some specific needs of others to which teenagers can respond? List them.

What are some specific activities teenagers can do to help meet these needs? List them.

What can teenagers learn about being good citizens from these activities? Describe.

Think of two specific incidents in which teenagers have become better citizens as a result of helping others. These may be personal experiences. Describe these examples in detail, including what the teenagers did and how it helped make them better citizens.

Once our students have answered these and similar questions, they have more than enough details to develop paragraphs for each of their reasons. Even more important, our students have learned a strategy for thinking through an issue and for generating data to support their ideas.

To get our students started, we suggest that they begin each paragraph of the body of the letter with a statement of one reason. We tell them they can organize the details in any way that seems appropriate to them. To demonstrate, we ask a student to put his or her details for one reason on the board. Then, on the overhead transparency we organize the details into a paragraph. Marcia organ-ized Jim's data arguing that students planning to go to college need to work as many hours as possible to help finance their college educations:

Most students I know who want to go to college don't have parents who can afford to send them. That means the only way for these kids to get an education is for them to pay a large part of the tuition and expenses themselves. My parents have five children; they can barely make ends meet now, much less send any of us to college. That's one reason my brother and I work as many hours as we do each week. Our money buys our clothes, pays for our entertainment, and goes in our college fund. I work forty hours a week at my job and put at least half of it in my savings account. I feel very good knowing that if I continue to work as many hours as I have been, I will be able to pay most of my college expenses, if I go to a state school. However, if this law limiting the hours I can work stands, I will not be able to save the money I need for college.

Marcia asked her class what they noticed about this paragraph. They identified the personal nature of the details and questioned the use of "I." She assured them that it is the personal nature of the argument that makes the "I" effective and that she encouraged personal anecdotes in persuasive writing. Because no one mentioned it, she asked them what held the paragraph together, what connected one detail with the next. They noticed the pronouns and the transitional word *however*, she pointed out that the repetition of key words also helped to connect ideas in this paragraph. Similarly, Ruth organized for her class the details from Doreen's statement of reasons.

Based on the details students have collected from answering the questions and from our modeling of the writing of a paragraph, they are ready to draft the bodies of their letters. For this purpose we take our classes to the computer room, where they will be working until the letters are completed. They rewrite their introductions, usually making revisions in the process, and then begin drafting the middle paragraphs. We move from student to student, answering questions, making occasional suggestions, solving minor computer problems, and encouraging them to argue for what they believe.

When the bodies of the letters have been drafted, we provide instruction on writing the concluding paragraph. Most students want simply to restate the introduction or write a summary; however, we want them to "conclude," to arrive at a solution to a problem, show a result, or make a recommendtion for action. To help her students in this task, Ruth asked the following questions about community service:

Have you agreed or disagreed with the school board's proposal to require 120 hours of community service for graduation from high school?

(Students who agreed answered the following questions:

What could be the benefits to our community of student involvement in community service? Briefly list the benefits.

What could be the benefits to the students themselves of their involvement in community service?

What action do you recommend?

(Students who disagreed answered the following questions:

What could be the problems to our town if students were forced to do community service in order to graduate? List them.

What could be the difficulties to students if forced to do community service? List them.

What action do you recommend?

Guided by the questions, Doreen wrote the following conclusion to he letter:

Because I believe community service is such a good idea, I support the Board's requirement of 120 hours of community service for graduation. The community will be a better place for all of us to live in and students will gain an understanding of what it means to be a good citizen. Therefore, I urge you to vote yes on this proposal.

Once the drafts of the essays have been completed, Marcia's class sends its papers to Ruth's class to be critiqued, and Ruth's class sends its papers to Marcia's class. To facilitate a productive review of the papers, we provide the following critique sheet:

Introduction
What is the problem being addressed?
What position has the writer taken?

What reasons has the writer stated to support that position?

What, if anything, do you suggest the writer add to the introduction to make a stronger case for his or her position?

Body
What is the topic of the first body paragraph?

What specific details support that topic?

What details, if any, don't help the writer develop this reason?

What additional details do you suggest to strengthen the argument?

What is the topic of the second body paragraph?

What specific details support that topic?

What details, if any, don't help the writer develop this reason?

What additional details do you suggest to strengthen the argument?

What is the topic of the third body paragraph?

What specific details support that topic?

What details, if any, don't help the writer develop this reason?

What additional details do you suggest to strengthen the argument?

Conclusion
Did the writer restate his or her position on the issue?

What benefits or problems did the writer discuss?

What result and recommendation for action did the writer present?

What, if anything, would you suggest the writer add to make the conclusion more convincing?

Personal Response
What did this paper add to your understanding of the issue?

We read the papers and the critique sheets and add our own comments and suggestions to those of the student reviewer. Then we return the papers to the writers, who read the critique sheets, review their papers and revise them, and take note of all the suggestions. We collect the final copies and the critiqued drafts. Rating the papers is fast and easy. We read them holistically and assign grades. Doreen's paper on community service is characteristic of the work students produce:

Because I believe community service is such a good idea, I support the Board's requirement that high school students volunteer 120 hours of their time over the four years of high school to community service in order to graduate. If this proposal is approved, I think the community will become a better place for all of us to live in. We as students will take more pride in our community as a result of our work. Most important, we will gain an understanding of what it means to be a good citizen. Our town will be more attractive as a result of students' involvement in civic improvement. Right now, there seems to be   no money to maintain the flower gardens in front of the the library. As a result, the area looks ugly and doesn't make people want to go inside. Students could easily take care of these gardens by planting pretty flowers and keeping them weeded. The community center needs painting very   badly. In fact, nobody likes to go there because the peeling paint is so depressing. A group of students could fix this in no time. I bet we could even get the local hardware store to donate the paint and equipment. Even though taking care of the gardens and painting the community center sounds like a lot of work, I know I would enjoy working on projects like these with my friends. We would have fun.

Everybody knows that when you do a job well you feel good about yourself. If we students help make our community more attractive, we will take pride in what we have done and in our town. People will want to come to our town and shop in local stores. In addition, other people will admire our work and start to feel better about teenagers. They will see that we aren't just troublemakers but can do good things too.

Working together with other people to make our community a better place in which to live will help us see ourselves as good citizens. We will learn just how much our town depends on the people who live in it to keep it going. So many jobs in towns like ours rely on volunteers. For example, meals on wheels depends on volunteer drivers to take food to elderly home bound residents. The local hospital relies on candystripers to man the telephones, move patients around, deliver flowers and gifts and newspapers. The daycare center depends on volunteers to read to the children and help on the playground. These are only a few of the services people in our town donate as good citizens. Students too can do all of these jobs as well as anyone else and share in the satisfaction of helping others.

Because I believe community service is important for our town and ourselves, I urge you to approve the proposed requirement that teenagers volunteer 120 hours of their time to community service. As a result, we will all benefit. We will have a better town, one in which we can take pride. And students will feel important because they will have done something worthwhile for their community.

We have been focusing on issues that affect students directly. We now want to involve them in issues that affect the community at large and to have a change of pace from the writing of persuasive essays. To determine what these issues are, we begin by asking our students to read the local newspaper for one week and cut out articles that refer to community concerns. In the meantime we have collected an assortment of articles related to issues affecting the town. Students bring their articles to class, and each student identifies the local issues currencly in the news. We list these issues on the board. Of course there is some overlapping, which we also note. Students usually mention

- Location of group homes
- Affordable housing
- Influx of illegal aliens
- Problems of the homeless
- Increased crime
- Increased taxes
- Impact of school budget cuts
- Impact of community budget cuts

Once we have identified the impact of pressing current issues in our town, we ask the students to identify five or six issues for the class to explore. To facilitate that exploration, we invite appropriate spokespersons from the community to address our classes. We instruct our students to take notes on what they hear, and we encourage them to ask questions. We tell them that taking notes will not only facilitate their listening but also be useful later on in their study of these issues.

Because the topic of providing housing for the homeless was an issue our students recently identified, we invited a representative from A-HOME to tell about the work of this private organization committed to creating housing for the homeless. She described the population her organization served, the sources of funding, and the opportunities available for community involvement. Obviously she was very much in favor of our town providing housing for the homeless. However, not all of our students agreed, and some of them challenged her to prove that the homeless deserved or even needed help. Whether or not she convinced our students to accept her position, she did provide them with considerable factual information.

We also invited the police chief to talk about crime in our area, the town supervisor to report on the impact of state budget cuts on local services, a clergyman to tell about the growing number of illegal aliens in our area, and a social worker to discuss the need for group homes in our community.

Once our students have heard the presentations, we invite them to create "docu-dramas" illustrating one position on an issue. We divide the class into five groups, one for each issue. As we have done before, we place signs about each issue around the room and invite students to select the issue of greatest interest to them to work on. If we get too many students in one group, we divide the group in half to enable all the students interested in that issue to work on it. Each group's first task is to agree on a position to take on the issue. Often this generates heated discussion. Because the issues students have identified are of such personal concern to them, they have strong feelings on one side or the other. The group members may not all agree on the position, which means that they must discuss their differences until they can arrive at a consensus. This procedure may take an entire class period, and sometimes one member of the group may have to compromise his or her position for the sake of the group's task. When this happens, we point out to the students that talking through a difficult issue, respecting other people's opinions, and arriving at some kind of agreement for the sake of action are necessary skills for success in life.

Once the groups have decided on their positions on the various issues, they are ready to plan their dramatic presentations. We call them *docu-dramas* because we want them to use the information they have gathered from the guest speakers, their reading, and any of their own experiences related to the issue. To get them started, we brainstorm with the class on possible scenarios for dramatizing their positions. We list the situations suggested by our students and offer a few of our own. These include such suggestions as

- Students arguing in the cafeteria
- A family discussion at the dinner table
- A homeless family trying to find a place to live
- A protest demonstration
- A day in the life of an illegal alien or a homeless person
- An incident involving a policeman
- An incident involving a landlord
- A school board meeting
- An incident involving a home owner
- An incident involving a local shop owner

We don't want to provide detailed suggestions for dramatizations because that limits the creativity of the groups. We allow three class sessions for students to invent their scenarios and prepare their dramatizations. This involves writing the script, blocking the action, assigning the parts, and rehearsing the docu-drama.

On presentation day we combine our classes. Our students enjoy performing for each other and discovering the different ways other groups have dealt with their issues. To conclude the activity, our students describe in their journals the effects of the project about their beliefs on these issues. Matt wrote:

> I always hated the homeless. I felt they got just what they deserved, were a bunch of deadbeats. I still think that's true of a lot of them, but I was really upset when I found out how many little children don't have homes. I mean that could be me out there or my baby sister! When we had to come to a decision in our group on the issue of homelessness, I had a real hard time. I argued and argued but finally I had to back down and let the group present a sympathetic picture of a homeless family. I played a young kid who had no shoes and so I couldn't go to school and everybody made fun of me. It's strange, but playing that kid changed me in a way. I really got into it. I saw for the first time that there was nothing that kid could do to change things and that being homeless wasn't his fault but he was stuck. That isn't fair and it got me mad. I now think the town has to do more to help homeless people help themselves.

So far in our study we have looked at the trials and tribulations of people in real life. These real-life situations help our disenchanted students relate to the kinds of problems characters encounter in literature. Because reading is an activity that requires us to imagine, it is often difficult for disenchanted students who are not experienced readers to have any tolerance for make-believe people. Because the students have dramatized some real-life problems in the preceding activities, they are better prepared to identify with fictional characters. We choose *Of Mice and Men* because the characters are so realistically drawn that the novel is accessible even to the most resistant students.

First we ask students to think about what it is like to be entirely alone. We turn out the lights and draw the shades and have the students close their eyes and imagine themselves totally alone. We ask

- Where are you?
- What are you thinking?
- What are you doing?
- How do you feel?
- What is the color of being alone?
- What is the temperature?

After at least five minutes of silence, we tell them to open their eyes and record their experiences briefly in their journals. Again, we ask where they were while they were alone? What were they thinking, doing, feeling? What colors do they associate with aloneness? What temperature? We give them 5–10 minutes to write, and we write as well.

We then ask them to share their journals with the class. As they do, we record their various thoughts in two separate lists, one focusing on the positive aspects of being alone and the other on the loneliness. Our students mention the peace and quiet of being alone, the pleasure of being able to think, and the space being alone gives them. However, most of them confess to being very frightened about being alone; they find it threatening. The colors of being alone are usually blues and blacks, and the temperature cold, even freezing.

We introduce *Of Mice and Men* as a story about people who are alone and ask students as they read this book to remember how they felt about being alone. We read the first few pages aloud and tell our students to listen for details that reveal something about the relationship between the two men. We ask them to decide if they are really friends or rather two people essentially alone though together? We also ask them to listen for clues about the personalities of the two men.

After we finish reading, we then ask students to go back over the section, reread it, and make notes about the two men described. We encourage them to work in pairs. They notice that one man, later identified as Lennie, is a huge hulk of a man, constantly compared to a bear; that he seems to lack control of his limbs; that he has a slack, expressionless face; and that he imitates everything the other man, George, does. They also notice that George is described as small and quick, with alert eyes and foresight, and seems to take care of the larger man. They quickly decide that something must be wrong with the other one, that he must be slow. They also wonder why the two travel together when all George can seem to do is get impatient and yell at Lennie.

Once students have an initial impression of George and Lennie, we tell them to finish reading the first chapter silently, looking for an answer to their question about why the two men travel together. When they finish reading the chapter, we ask them to write their thoughts about what they have learned in their journals. Marissa wrote:

I think George yells at Lennie too much. He can't help it if he is slow. He really makes Lennie feel bad always threatening to leave him and telling him how great he could have it if only Lennie weren't in the way. I don't really like George at all.

Jeff wrote:

It's easy to see why George gets fed up with Lennie. He really is incredibly dumb, but I don't really think he is all that mean to him. They keep talking about this dream they have and George cares about it too. George must get something out of being with Lennie or he wouldn't put up with him so long. I'm sure losing that job in Weed because of Lennie wasn't the first time they got in trouble because of him.

Once students have read and reacted personally to the opening chapter, we assign them the next chapter as homework. We prepare them for their reading by telling them they will be meeting a number of people George and Lennie work with in their new job. They should pay particular attention to one couple: a jealous husband named Curley and his wife (who for some reason is called only "Curley's wife"), an old physically challenged man named Candy, and an African American man called Crooks. We ask them to remember what happened to George and Lennie in Weed and to think for a few moments before they predict what will happen in the new job. They usually are able to predict some kind of trouble with Curley over his wife, and they expect some kind of racial trouble. Before they leave class, we tell them that as they read we want them to write down what they notice about the people they meet, particularly Candy, Crooks, Curley, and his wife.

The next day we discuss these impressions. They usually comment on the prejudice shown Crooks, the suspicion the relationship of George and Lennie generates, the pugnaciousness of Curley (they don't like him very much and can't understand why he always wants to pick a fight), and the inappropriate flirtatiousness of Curley's wife. They also feel that their predictions were right on target. They are sure there will be trouble between Curley and the others over his wife, and they point out Lennie's fears of staying at this new job when he says, "I don' like this place, George. This ain't a good place. I wanna get outta here."

After students share their impressions of the characters, we begin to read Chapter 3 aloud. We have the students portray the characters, reading the story as a play. Because *Of Mice and Men* has so much dialogue, this approach works very well. We usually read the narrative sections. We read as far as the killing by Carlson of Candy's dog. Then we ask students to assume the persona of Candy and write in their journals, expressing his thoughts and feelings when Carlson takes Candy's dog out to shoot it and he lies silently on his bunk staring at the ceiling. We allow 10–15 minutes for these persona journals. Before sharing the results, we ask students to add a section in their own voice about how *they* feel about what has occurred. We share those reactions first. Most of our students are very moved by the killing of the dog. They feel sorry for Candy, but they understand the men's desire to get rid of such a smelly old animal. After they have expressed their personal views, we share the journals. Karen wrote:

> What am I gonna do now? That dog was everythin' to me. I'm all alone now. Why'd they hafta go an kill him? He warn't hurtin nobody. He slept most of the time and I took care of him. He was all I got. Now I got noth-in. They'd probably like to shoot me too when I get old and smelly enuf! I don't want ta ever talk to any of them agin, never agin.

When they write in Candy's voice, students are able to express much greater sympathy for him than they usually do in their personal-reaction journals. This assignment generates a conversation about the problems of growing old, feeling helpless and totally alone. We try to sensitize students to ways they can help the older people in their own lives to feel less alone and to make them feel they still have dignity.

We then assign the rest of Chapter 3 for homework, asking students to watch for (and record in their notebooks) details of George and Lennie's dream and any new developments regarding that dream, as well as the details of a major problem between Curley and Lennie. In class the next day students want to discuss Lennie's strength and their amusement at what happens to Curley when he picks on Lennie. They can't believe Lennie is *so* slow he can't stop crushing Curley's hand until George instructs him to do so.

Once their fascination with the fight has been satisfied, we focus the discussion on George and Lennie's dream. We speculate on the possibility of their achieving it. This often leads to a discussion of the relative importance of just having a dream, even if it is not attainable. We talk about why having a place of one's own is so important. Candy is willing to invest all his disability money if George and Lennie will let him be part of their dream. Crooks even offers to work for nothing if they will let him in on it. To our students their dream seems very modest. They can't imagine having a dream like that.

Because students refer to their own dreams, we ask them to describe those dreams in their journals. They get very involved with this activity and usually insist on being allowed more than the usual 15 minutes to write. So we give them the time they need, usually no more than 25 minutes. If there is time left in the period, we let them form groups of four to share their journal entries. This sharing generates considerable laughter and conversation. Many of them envision themselves as very rich, with palatial estates and gorgeous cars, living without having to work and being on a perpetual vacation.

Before we continue reading, we tell our students they will be writing a persona journal as Crooks imagining how they would feel if they were treated as he is in Chapter 4. We assign parts and read aloud, making no comment on the events but letting the power of the narrative speak for itself. Once we complete the reading, we ask students to begin to write their persona journals, describing Crooks's feelings and thoughts about his encounter with Lennie and with Curley's wife. Students are told to complete the entry for homework and to comment as themselves about this chapter.

The next time we meet, students are very eager to share their responses and their persona journals. Alicia, who felt very sympathetic with Crooks, wrote:

> All my life, that's the way it's been—all my life. I never had anyone. Couldn't even play with the other kids. We was the only colored family in town. I got my books but books ain't no good. I wisht I was George. At least he has Lennie. It wouldn't matter that he didn't unnerstand me. It's the talkin'. D...n that slut. Who does she think she is anyway, comin' in here; she's got no right. I got to have at least this little space for myself. Don't they see I got feelin's too? I jus' want them all to get outa here, to leave me alone. It's no use hopin' about joinin' George and them guys; it'll never work, jus' get me all worked up agin, hopin', gettin' hurt.

Like Alicia, our students are struck by the cruelty and insensitivity of the characters to each other. Crooks is mistreated just because he is African-American, and he is made to feel like nothing by the girl. But she also is mistreated and made to feel unwelcome, and students express some sympathy for her desire for companionship. They also notice that even Crooks enjoys mistreating someone else, in this case Lennie, teasing him unmercifully about the possibility that George will abandon him. We ask students to find the passages that were most powerful for them. Most of them focus on the confrontation between Crooks and the girl and the way in which she makes him feel like nothing. Crooks gets upset and tries to get Curley's wife to leave his room:

> "You got no rights comin' in a colored man's room. You got no rights messing around in here at all. Now you jus' get out, ann'get out quick. If you don't I'm gonna ast the boss not to ever let you come in the barn no more."
>
> She turned on him in scorn. "Listen, N———r," she said. "You know what I can do to you if you open your trap?"
>
> Crooks stared hopelessly at her, and then he sat down on his bunk and drew into himself.
>
> She closed on him. "You know what I could do?"
>
> Crooks seemed to grow smaller, and he pressed himself against the wall. "Yes, ma'am."
>
> "Well, you keep your place then, N———r. I could get you strung up on a tree so easy it ain't even funny."
>
> Crooks had reduced himself to nothing. There was no personality, no ego—nothing to arouse either like or dislike. He said, "Yes, ma'am," and his voice was toneless.'

Our reading of this section of the book leads to a discussion of prejudice in our own community and school. We ask students to think of a time when they or someone they know was excluded or made to feel unwanted because of who they are—whether it was a result of their religion, their racial background, their gender, or their age. They write about the experience and how they felt. Stephen, a student who recently transferred from an inner-city school, wrote about his experiences in a predominantly white community:

> Me and my brothers went to the movies one night. We bought our tickets and started to go inside. But this guy, I guess he was the manager, comes out and says "what do you think you're doin'?" We weren't doing anything, we just wanted to go to the movies and we told him that. He made us show him our tickets. Then he said, "You Black b———s better keep your noses clean. I don't want no trouble from you." We went into the movie but we didn't have any fun. My brothers said we should of said something, but I just wanted to go home. I felt sick.

We then ask our students to work in groups of four, share their experiences, and talk in general about why people treat each other in prejudicial ways and what they can do about it when it occurs in school or in their community. When Stephen told what had happened to him, his group was indignant and wanted to report the manager to the theater owner. Their reaction reflects the effectiveness of this activity in helping students begin to recognize the prejudice around them and to empathize with the pain of those who experience prejudice. By writing as Crooks, by seeing the prejudice against Lennie, Curley's wife, and even Candy, and by rethinking an experience they have had with prejudice, our students become a little more sensitive to the feelings of other people.

They are now ready to complete the reading of the book on their own. We ask them to predict what will happen. They know a great deal about all the people; they have seen the conflicts between them; they know that Lennie is potentially a source of trouble. They write very briefly, predicting the ending. José wrote:

> I bet there's going to be another big fight. Curley and Lennie have already gone at it once. Curley isn't the kind of guy to just let it go at that. He's going to want revenge somehow. And, I can't quite figure how the girl will fit in but the fight's got to have something to do with her. Maybe she decides to run off with Lennie and Curley catches them and shoots them both dead and George gets so mad at Curley he kills him and then George gets strung up by a lynch mob. Something like that.

Students read Chapters 5 and 6 for homework (usually over a weekend). They come to class eager to talk about the ending. Everyone has an opinion. Students write an end-of-book reaction journal. Many of them are very displeased with the ending. They want George and Lennie to get their farm with the rabbits and to live happily ever after. They can't figure out why George shot Lennie. Many are very angry at him. We reread the last few pages of the book to see if we can resolve the "problem." We read to the students, this time emphasizing the pain George exhibits and his reluctance to take the action he does. Many students see the parallel with Candy's dog and Lennie. They point out that Candy always regretted not killing his dog himself; perhaps Lennie is seen by George as "his dog" and that is why he kills him. This doesn't satisfy everyone, however, because other students insist Lennie is a human being, not a dog, and no one has the right to take another person's life.

The controversy is always lively and leads us to suggest that the only way to resolve these differences is to have a trial. The question of course is whom to hold responsible for the deaths of Curley's wife and Lennie. Rather than dictate who should be the defendant, we leave the choice to our students. For this purpose the class is divided into four groups. Each group is to try to make a case that one of the major characters is responsible for the tragedy in the story and deserves to be punished by the law. Signsare placed around the room for each possible defen-dant (George, Lennie, Curley, and the girl). Students choose groups based on who they feel is most responsible for the tragedy.

The students respond enthusiastically to the task of convincing the rest of the class to indict their character. For an entire class period they work diligently on their arguments, with one student acting as recorder.

The next day a presenter from each group argues for the indictment of her or his character. In one of Ruth's classes Leslie said:

> The whole thing was Curley's fault. He kept attacking Lennie. He was such a terrible husband that Curley's wife had no choice but to find company where she could, putting her in a position where Lennie would be alone with her. Lennie wasn't responsible for what he did; he never meant to hurt anyone or anything but he couldn't control his own strength. It was Curley that organized the posse that went after Lennie making George's choice one of letting Curley find Lennie and do what he wanted with him or killing Lennie himself, no choice at all.

Arthur made a case for the girl being the real problem:

> She was a real slut. Every time she went near anyone she was trouble. She had no business being in the barn that day; she knew how jealous her husband was. She had a husband. Why was she messing with other guys. It's all her fault.

Daryl wanted to indict Lennie:

> Lennie is a menace to society. It's one thing to say he is not able to control his strength; it's another to allow him to run around loose killing anyone who happens to have the bad luck to be alone with him and have soft hair for him to stroke. Something has to be done about dudes like Lennie.

Maribel was most incensed at George:

> He murdered his best friend. How can we let him get away with cold blood-
> ed murder? He had choices. He could have run away with him again just
> like he did after the problem in Weed. He could have allowed them to
> capture him and insisted he get professional help rather than be put on
> trial for Curley's wife's death. What kind of a country is this when people
> take the law into their own hands and get away with it? He's a real loser.

After all the presenters have made their cases, we take a class vote by secret ballot. While there is some loyalty to the original group, many of the students are independent enough to be moved by the arguments of an opposing
presenter. Finally the decision is made to try one of the characters; more often
than not, George is put on trial for the murder of Lennie.

We ask for volunteers to play the various roles: We need three lawyers and
three witnesses for each side, a judge, a bailiff, two court stenographers to keep
track of the proceedings, and two expert witnesses to keep the trial from changing the text of the story too much. The rest of the class becomes the jury. We
want everyone to be involved in productive activity, but the preparatory work load
is uneven. To enhance the work of the jury, we have them work with the two
experts and the judge to draw up a list of facts not subject to interpretation from
which the two sides may not deviate during the course of the trial. Our students'
experiences in writing persuasive essays help them distinguish between what is
fact and what is opinion. The experts first have to review the story carefully so
they can know whether testimony being given is faithful to the novel. Then they
draw up their set of facts. At the same time, the judge works out his own set of
facts. The jury also works independently to develop a set of facts. Finally they
meet to reconcile their lists and agree on one definitive list. One of Marcia's
classes agreed to these facts:

> Lennie is retarded.
> Lennie and George travel together.
> Lennie killed the mouse, the dog and Curley's wife.
> George killed Lennie.

Finally the judge and the two experts confer with the lawyers and debate
each "fact." No fact can be admitted into the final fact book unless all parties
agree. Several minor adjustments usually have to be made to eliminate certain
"facts" that are not acceptable to one of the lawyers. For example, while it is
true that Curley's wife goes into the barn of her own free will, it is not considered a fact that she has no business being in the barn alone with Lennie.

With a fact book like this, neither side can make a claim that can not be
substantiated by reference to the original text, at least on these basic facts. They
can't decide that Lennie committed suicide, for example.

After completing their fact book, the jury meets with a social studies or law
teacher who acquaints them with trial procedure and California criminal law
of the 1940s and shares some materials on similar cases with them.

While the jury and the experts are preparing for the trial, the witnesses are reviewing the book to get to know their characters well enough to respond appro-priately to the questions they will be asked. They are instructed to draw up affidavits to submit to the judge and to the lawyers of both sides. The affidavits include

- Who they are.
- Their role in the events leading to Lennie's death.
- Their thoughts about the charges based on their knowledge of what occurred.

Witnesses also are responsible for writing down the questions they would like to be asked and then meeting with the lawyers for their side to make a final determination of what questions they will actually be asked. Once they have determined the questions, they work out tentative answers to the questions so as to be both truthful and helpful to their side. The final step of witness preparation involves trying to anticipate with their lawyers the cross-examination questions and devising strategies for answering possible questions.

The major efforts fall on the lawyers of course. They have to prepare a brief, consisting of a one-to two-page summary of the strategy they will employ to prosecute or defend against each of the charges and the testimony they expect to elicit from each of the witnesses; the questions for each witness; an opening statement; and a closing statement. We require that they submit to us before the trial begins at least the strategy statement. We want to know who will do what and how each side intends to try to convince the jury of the truth of its position. We also monitor the preparation for the trial carefully to make sure that the lawyers have thought through the questions they will ask and are ready on opening day with a formal opening statement.

We allow at least five class periods for the preparation of the trial and at least three periods for the actual trial. On trial day we invite the principal and other interested staff to attend the proceedings. When possible, we hold class in the room that has been remodeled as a courtroom and where our student court tries its   cases. We embellish our trial with as many formalities as possible to give added weight to what we are doing. Our judge wears a judicial robe (usually a black graduation robe contributed by Ruth); we have a judge's gavel (the bigger and more impressive the better); the bailiff has everyone rise as she announces the arrival of the judge and calls the court to order; and we formally swear all witnesses in using a copy of *Of Mice and Men* in place of the usual Bible. All students, but especially disenchanted students, are intrigued and amused by this pomp and ceremony.

While the trial is taking place, the jury takes notes on what is happening. We instruct them that these notes will be collected as part of the final reports they will write about their verdicts.

The trial is always very exciting. The lawyers take their task seriously and present eloquent opening statements. The witnesses play their roles to the hilt, even quoting at times from their words in the book. Most impressive is the degree of involvement from the entire class. Sometimes several of the jurors get so involved that they feel the lawyers aren't doing a good enough job, so they question witnesses or even switch from the jury to the team helping the lawyers of one side or the other present their case. Because concern for improving their critical reading and thinking skills is more important than adhering to strict trial procedure, we permit these liberties to be taken—indeed, we even encourage them.

At the end of the trial student performers are applauded by the rest of the class. We then dismiss the lawyers and the witnesses and send them to the library so we can meet with the jury alone. In the library students work on the reports that represent their written contribution to the trial. We grade students based on an assessment of their effort in preparing their roles, their performance during the trial, and on the final written reports. The lawyers firm up their written briefs, including their opening and closing statements, the logic of their presentations and the questions they had asked each witness. They also analyze their perform-ance and how the trial went, second-guessing themselves on what questions they wish they had asked and what they would have done differently if they had it to do over again. The witnesses write in the personae they had played, explaining why they had testified either for or against the defendant and repeating the gist of their personal position. They also analyze how they feel the trial went and what they wish they had had a chance to say that could have helped their side make a better case. The experts use their knowledge of the story to predict the verdict and critique the trial.

The judge and jury meet to reach a verdict. Each juror writes down his or her verdict on each of the charges and the reasons for the decision, citing specific points raised by each side and specific testimony. The judge does the same. Then each jury member gets an opportunity to read her or his initial finding. (For propriety's sake, the judge keeps his initial views to himself.) Usually there is considerable disparity of views. The judge acts as discussion facilitator as the jurors attempt to reach a consensus on a verdict. Jury deliberations are often difficult and take at least a full class period. It is important to allow enough time because students are learning a great deal about argumentation, persuasion, compromise, and group dynamics from this exercise. They also take their roles very seriously and resent being rushed to a verdict.

At some point we have to call a halt to deliberations even if a unanimous verdict has not been reached. We poll the jury and declare a hung jury if necessary. Jurors are then instructed to write a one-or two-page rationale for the final verdict. They include an analysis of each side's argument and make suggestions for improving each side's case. We assess their efforts based on the notes they took on the trial, their skill in using specifics from the trial to explain their verdict, and their critiques of the trial.

We bring the class back together to hear the verdict read. The defendant stands as the judge reads the determination of the jury. If the defendant is found guilty, the judge defers sentencing until the next class period. Before sentencing, the defendant is given the opportunity to say a few final words. In passing sentence the judge summarizes the trial, the presentation of the evidence, and his or her reason for the particular sentence.

As a final activity, students write a letter to us relating their feelings about the trial and its effect on their response to the book. Chris wrote:

> I thought the trial was a neat idea. I really got into being a lawyer. I thought I'd be afraid to get up in front of the class and do all that, but I forgot about myself when John started getting all spastic about how terrible George was to kill Lennie. I only thought about how I could convince everybody that George had no choice. He didn't want to hurt Lennie. He just knew if he didn't do something, Curley would torture him or worse. I think they really stretched things when they put Crooks on the stand against George. Really, he was the perfect witness for our side, but I guess they had to use somebody. Oh well. I think you should use this again next year, but tell the kids when they are reading the book that they will be having a trial at the end. I would have read the book more carefully maybe and even taken some notes if I had known I was going to need so many specifics. At the end, it's hard to find the right pages and stuff. Anyway, it really was fun. I hope we do more projects like this one.

"Trials and Tribulations" helps students work through the "best and worst of times" in their lives by giving them a sense of empowerment over the complex issues that affect them. The activities of this unit afford them an opportunity to discover ways to use language to effect changes in themselves and their world. They learn to support positions on issues with reasons and specifics. They argue, persuade, compromise, and assess their own efforts. In addition, they see the relevance of literature to their own experiences and dilemmas. They examine problems of prejudice, sexism, aging, and euthanasia and become aware of the difficulties of decision-making and the pitfalls inherent in making value judgments. In short, "Trials and Tribulations" helps prepare our students for the complexities they encounter in their own lives.

Bibliography

Some of the works that have influenced our classroom strategies:

Atwell, Nancie. *In the Middle: Writing, Reading, and Learning with Adolescents.* Portsmouth, NY: Boynton/Cook, 1987.

Berthoff, Ann E. *Forming, Thinking, Writing.* Portsmouth, NH: Boynton/Cook, 1988..

Britton, James. *Prospect and Retrospect.* Portsmouth, NH: Heinemann, Boynton/Cook, 1982.

_____ *English Language Arts Syllabus, K-12.* Albany, NY: The State Education Department, 1988.

Fulwiler, Toby. *Teaching with Writing.* Portsmouth, NH: Boynton/Cook, 1987.

Goswami, Dixie and Peter Stillman. *Reclaiming the Classroom.* Portsmouth, NH: Boynton/Cook, 1987.

Johnson, David W., and Roger T. Johnson. *Cooperative Learning.* New Brighton, MN: Interaction Book Company, 1984.

Kirby, Don and Tom Liner. *Inside Out.* Portsmouth, NH: Heinemann, Boynton/Cook, 1988.

Murray, Donald. *Writing Your Way.* New York, NY: Holt, Rinehart, and Winston. 1984..

Murray, Donald. *Read to Write.* New York, NY: Holt, Rinehart, and Winston, 1986.

Rockas, Leo. *Ways In, Analyzing and Responding to Literature.* Portsmouth, NH: Boynton/Cook, 1984.

Rosenblatt, Louise M. *The Reader, the Text, the Poem.* Carbondale, IL: Southern Illinois University Press, 1978.

Smith, Frank. *Joining the Literacy Club.* Portsmouth, NH: Heinemann, 1988.

Stillman, Peter. *Writing Your Way.* Portsmouth, NH: Boynton/Cook, 1984.

Zemelman, Steven and Harvey Daniels. *A Community of Writers.* Portsmouth, NH: Heinemann, 1988.

Afterword

The integrated English/language arts classroom has been described as a place where teachers enable students to explore and expand their linguistic powers in an atmosphere that is comfortable, satisfying, and relevant to their lives. That is the kind of classroom we strive to create and have described in *English for the Disenchanted*.

Our units reflect a student-centered philosophy in which the teacher functions as instructor, facilitator, model, resource, and evaluator. Therefore, instruction is determined by the needs of the students. Our lessons are designed to enable students to take charge of their own learning; our strategies include modeling the skills we want our students to develop and providing the resources they need to achieve these skills; and our evaluation practices include student self-assessment as a vital part of learning. In short, our classroom strategies are dictated by our determination of the language needs, personal interests, and academic abilities of our students.

What we present in each chapter is meant to reflect this educational philosophy in terms of some of our specific classroom practices. Our descriptions are not meant to be prescriptive but to serve as models of what you can do in your classroom. And, we encourage you to experiment with and adapt our materials to the specific needs of your students, and we invite you to share with us your experiences in using our lessons with your disenchanted students.